GCSE History is always topical with CGP...

Edexcel's "Early Elizabethan England, 1558-88" topic for GCSE History can seem harder than the Spanish Armada — but with this CGP Topic Guide, you'll sail through it!

It's packed with crystal-clear notes, plenty of helpful activities, sample answers, exam tips, exam-style questions and more. Other History books are just pretenders to the throne.

CGP — still the best! ☺

Our sole aim here at CGP is to produce the highest quality books — carefully written, immaculately presented and dangerously close to being funny.

Then we work our socks off to get them out to you — at the cheapest possible prices.

Published by CGP

Editors:
Izzy Bowen, Robbie Driscoll, Harry Millican and Holly Robinson.

Contributors:
Peter Callaghan, Paddy Gannon.

With thanks to Charley Maidment and Jack Tooth for the proofreading.
With thanks to Emily Smith for the copyright research.

Acknowledgements:

Cover image: Queen Elizabeth I (1533-1603) being carried in Procession (Eliza Triumphans) c.1601 (oil on canvas), Peake, Robert (fl.1580-1626) (attr. to) / Private Collection / Bridgeman Images

With thanks to Mary Evans for permission to use the images on pages 6, 16, 22, 26, 32 and 42.

Coat of arms image on page 12. © Sodacan. Licensed under the Creative Commons Attribution-ShareAlike 3.0 Unported license https://creativecommons.org/licenses/by-sa/3.0/deed.en

ISBN: 978 1 78908 290 6
Printed by Elanders Ltd, Newcastle upon Tyne.
Clipart from Corel®

Based on the classic CGP style created by Richard Parsons.

Contents

Exam Skills

Queen, Government and Religion, 1558-1569

Challenges at Home and Abroad, 1569-1588

Elizabethan Society in the Age of Exploration, 1558-1588

Exam Hints and Tips

You'll have to take three papers in Edexcel GCSE History. This book will help you with Paper 2, Booklet B.

You will take 3 Papers altogether

1) Paper 1 is 1 hour 15 minutes long. It's worth 52 marks — 30% of your GCSE. This paper will be divided into 2 sections:
- Section A: Historic Environment.
- Section B: Thematic Study.

It's really important that you make sure you know which topics you're studying for each paper.

2) Paper 2 is 1 hour 45 minutes long. It's worth 64 marks — 40% of your GCSE. This paper will be divided into two question and answer booklets:
- Booklet P: Period Study.
- Booklet B: British Depth Study.

This book covers the British Depth Study Early Elizabethan England, 1558-88.

3) Paper 3 is 1 hour 20 minutes long. It's worth 52 marks — 30% of your GCSE. This paper will be divided into 2 sections, both about a Modern Depth Study:
- Section A: 2 questions, one of which is based on a source.
- Section B: A four-part question based on 2 sources and 2 interpretations.

Remember these Tips for Approaching the Questions

Organise your Time in the exam

1) In the exam, you'll have to answer three questions on Early Elizabethan England and three questions on your Period Study. It's important to stay organised so that you have time to answer all the questions.

2) The more marks a question is worth, the longer your answer should be.

3) Don't get carried away writing lots for a question that's only worth 4 marks — you'll need to leave time for the higher mark questions.

Try to leave a few minutes at the end of the exam to go back and read over your answers.

Always use a Clear Writing Style

1) Start a new paragraph for each new point you want to discuss.

2) Try to use clear handwriting and pay attention to spelling, grammar and punctuation.

Stay Focused on the question

1) Make sure that you answer the question. Don't just chuck in everything you know about the topic.

2) Think about what the key words are in the question. For longer questions, it's a good idea to scribble down a quick plan of your main points before you start writing. Cross through this neatly at the end so it isn't marked.

It might help to write the first sentence of every paragraph in a way that addresses the question, e.g. "Another reason why the Spanish Armada failed was..."

3) Your answers have got to be relevant and accurate — make sure you include precise details like the dates of plots and wars and the names of the people or groups involved in them.

Exam Hints and Tips

This page is all about the <u>British Depth Study</u>. There are <u>three questions</u> which <u>test two main skills</u>.

There are Three exam questions in the British Depth Study

1) The first question will ask you to <u>describe two features</u> of something — it might be an <u>event</u>, a <u>group of people</u> or another <u>significant aspect</u> from the period.

> Describe two aspects of Elizabeth's religious settlement of 1559.   [4 marks]

2) In the next question, you'll be asked to <u>explain</u> the <u>causes</u> of a specific <u>event</u> or <u>development</u>.

> Explain why the Revolt of the Northern Earls broke out.   [12 marks]

3) Finally, you'll need to answer <u>one</u> more question, from a choice of <u>two</u>. Each will give you a <u>statement</u> and you'll be asked <u>how far you agree</u> with it.

> 'The threats to Elizabeth's rule from abroad were more dangerous than the threats from at home.' How far do you agree? Explain your answer.   [16 marks]

4) In question types 2) and 3), you'll be given some <u>'stimulus points'</u> — hints about things you could include in your answer. You <u>don't</u> have to include details about these stimulus points, so <u>don't panic</u> if you can't remember much about them. Even if you do write about the stimulus points, you <u>must</u> add <u>other information</u> too — if you don't, you <u>can't</u> get full marks.

The British Depth Study tests Two Main Skills

Knowledge and Understanding

1) For <u>all the British Depth Study questions</u>, you'll get marks for showing <u>knowledge and understanding</u> of the <u>key features</u> of the topic.

2) You'll need to use <u>accurate</u> and <u>relevant</u> information to <u>support</u> your answers in the exam.

> The <u>Knowledge and Understanding</u> activities in this book will help you to revise the <u>important facts</u> about the period so that you have <u>plenty of information</u> to help you in the exam.

Thinking Historically

1) As well as knowing the <u>facts</u> about Early Elizabethan England, you'll also need to use <u>historical concepts</u> to <u>analyse</u> key events and developments. These concepts include <u>significance</u>, <u>continuity</u> and <u>change</u>, and <u>cause</u> and <u>consequence</u>.

2) You'll need to be able to find <u>links</u> between different events and explain <u>why</u> things happened the way they did.

3) You'll also need to use historical concepts to give a <u>judgement</u> on an issue. This may require you to explain how <u>important</u> you think a <u>person</u>, <u>event</u> or <u>development</u> was in Early Elizabethan England. You should do this by <u>weighing up</u> how important the topic in the question is against <u>other factors</u>.

> The <u>Thinking Historically</u> activities will help you understand the <u>causes</u> and <u>consequences</u> of different events, <u>similarities</u> and <u>differences</u> within the periods, and how far things <u>changed</u> or <u>stayed</u> the same in Early Elizabethan England.

No, not the Queen Elizabeth on the telly — the other one...

Early Elizabethan England was a pretty exciting time — lots of pirates, raids and dastardly plots. This book has all the key facts and will also help you practise the skills you'll need for the exam.

English Society and Government in 1558

In 1558, England had been governed by <u>Tudor monarchs</u> for more than seventy years. The country had <u>well-organised</u> systems of central and local government, but there were some major <u>divisions</u> in society.

Queen Elizabeth I was from the House of Tudor

The <u>Tudor family</u> had ruled England since Henry VII became king in 1485. Here's their family tree:

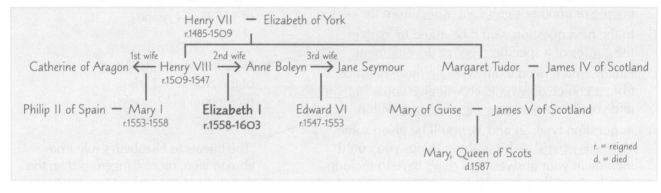

Elizabeth ruled with the Support of the Privy Council

1) Elizabeth was the most <u>powerful</u> figure in Elizabethan England. Everyone was expected to be <u>loyal</u> to the Queen and <u>obey</u> her.

2) The <u>Privy Council</u> was a group of around twenty of the Queen's most <u>trusted counsellors</u>. They <u>advised</u> her on all aspects of government and ensured her <u>wishes were carried out</u>. They were expected to obey her orders even if they disagreed with her.

3) <u>Parliament</u> was made up of members of the <u>nobility</u> and the <u>gentry</u>. The Queen needed Parliament's consent to pass <u>new laws</u> or <u>raise taxes</u>. Parliament only met when the Queen <u>summoned</u> it, and Elizabeth tried to <u>avoid using it</u> — she only called Parliament 13 times during her 44-year reign.

4) The Queen relied on members of the <u>nobility and gentry</u> to enforce <u>law and order</u> throughout the country. <u>Local government</u> posts like Justice of the Peace and sheriff were <u>unpaid</u>, but many men <u>volunteered</u> in order to increase their <u>local power</u> and <u>influence</u>. <u>Justices of the Peace</u> were particularly important — they enforced the law, provided for the poor and ensured roads and bridges were maintained.

Comment and Analysis

Elizabeth used <u>patronage</u> to ensure the <u>support</u> of the nobility and gentry. This often involved handing out <u>titles</u> and <u>offices</u> that gave the holder a source of <u>income</u>. Elizabeth distributed patronage <u>widely</u> to ensure that no-one felt left out — this helped to ensure <u>political stability</u>.

There were Social and Economic Divisions

1) England's <u>population</u> had been <u>rising</u> steadily since around 1500. Most people lived and worked in <u>rural areas</u>, but <u>towns and cities</u> were <u>growing</u> rapidly. <u>London</u> was by far the <u>largest</u> and most important city.

2) The economy was dominated by <u>agriculture</u>, but farming practices were <u>changing</u> (see p.44). The export of <u>woollen cloth</u> to <u>Europe</u> was very important to the economy, but merchants were also starting to explore trade with the <u>Americas</u> and <u>Asia</u> (see p.48-50).

3) Elizabethan society was dominated by a small, <u>land-owning aristocracy</u> of nobility and gentry. There was also a growing number of wealthy men who earned their living as <u>lawyers</u> or <u>merchants</u>.

4) There was great <u>inequality</u>, and the divide between rich and poor was growing. <u>Poverty</u> became a <u>major problem</u> in Elizabethan England (see p.44-46).

The <u>gentry</u> were part of the <u>social elite</u> in Elizabethan England, <u>below</u> the level of the <u>nobility</u>. Members of the gentry were people who <u>owned land</u> and lived off the <u>income</u> it provided. They <u>didn't</u> have to do other <u>work</u> to survive.

English Society and Government in 1558

Have a go at these activities to make sure you're familiar with Elizabethan society and government.

Knowledge and Understanding

1) Which four Tudor monarchs ruled England before Queen Elizabeth?
   Give the dates of their reigns.

2) Give three responsibilities of Justices of the Peace.

3) Put the following in order of their social importance, with the most important first.

   | lawyers and merchants | nobility | Queen Elizabeth | poor people | gentry |

4) What is meant by the term 'patronage'?

5) How did patronage benefit the following people?
   a) Queen Elizabeth
   b) the nobility and gentry

6) Explain how the following were changing during the 1500s. Give as much detail as you can.

   | a) England's population | b) the population of towns and cities | c) agriculture | d) overseas trade | e) social equality |

Thinking Historically

1) Copy and complete the table below about the different groups that were part
   of Queen Elizabeth's government. Include as much detail as you can.

	Privy Council	Parliament	Local government
a) Who was it made up of?			
b) What was its role?			

2) For each statement in the boxes below, write down evidence for and against it.

   | a) 'Elizabeth had limited power over the different parts of her government.' | b) 'Parliament had more power than local government.' | c) 'The Privy Council had a lot of influence over Elizabeth.' |

Elizabeth was very powerful, but she didn't rule alone...

To really ace the exam, you need to understand the key features of Elizabethan society and government. Make sure you know the role of the Queen, the Privy Council and Parliament.

Queen, Government and Religion, 1558-1569

The Challenges of a Female Monarch

Elizabeth I had a rocky start in life and faced some pretty <u>serious problems</u> when she first became queen.

Elizabeth I was Cautious, Intelligent and Powerful

© Mary Evans / Iberfoto

1) Elizabeth was <u>Henry VIII's</u> second child, the daughter of his second wife, <u>Anne Boleyn</u>. As a child, she was <u>third</u> in line to the throne (behind Edward VI and Mary I), so <u>no-one</u> really <u>expected</u> her to become queen.

2) Elizabeth had a <u>difficult upbringing</u> and sometimes <u>feared for her life</u>. In 1554, she was accused of <u>conspiring</u> against her half-sister, Queen Mary I, and placed under <u>house arrest</u> for almost a year.

3) Elizabeth was <u>very cautious</u> and only trusted a few <u>close advisers</u>. She could also be <u>indecisive</u> — she was reluctant to make decisions without carefully considering their possible <u>consequences</u>.

4) She was <u>intelligent</u>, <u>confident</u> and very <u>well educated</u>. Despite having had little training in how to govern, she became a <u>powerful and effective</u> leader.

Elizabeth faced many Difficulties when she became queen

She had been declared Illegitimate

1) In 1533, <u>Henry VIII</u> had <u>divorced</u> his first wife, Catherine of Aragon, and married Anne Boleyn. Divorce was <u>forbidden</u> in the <u>Catholic Church</u>, so many Catholics believed Henry's marriage to Anne was <u>not valid</u> and their daughter, Elizabeth, was <u>illegitimate</u>.

2) When Henry's marriage to Anne Boleyn was <u>dissolved</u> and Anne was <u>executed</u> in 1536, Henry declared Elizabeth <u>illegitimate</u>. Although Henry later <u>changed his mind</u> about this, some <u>Protestants</u> still questioned Elizabeth's <u>legitimacy</u>.

Comment and Analysis

The issue of Elizabeth's legitimacy <u>weakened</u> her claim to the throne and allowed others, especially <u>Mary, Queen of Scots</u> (see p.16), to claim that they had <u>more right</u> to rule.

People thought it was Unnatural for a Woman to be in charge

1) In the 16th century, most people believed the <u>monarch</u> should be a <u>man</u>. They thought that rule by a <u>woman</u> was <u>unnatural</u>. The <u>violence and chaos</u> of <u>Mary I's</u> reign had reinforced people's belief that women could not rule successfully.

2) Most people expected Elizabeth to act as a <u>figurehead</u>, without any real power. They thought she should let her <u>male counsellors</u> take control or find a <u>husband</u> to govern for her.

3) Elizabeth was <u>determined to rule</u> in her own right and <u>refused</u> to let her counsellors take over.

She was expected to Marry and produce an Heir

1) Because people believed women <u>couldn't rule effectively</u>, there was <u>pressure</u> for Elizabeth to find a <u>husband</u> who could rule for her.

2) There were also concerns about the <u>succession</u>. If Elizabeth died <u>without an heir</u>, there would be a risk of <u>civil war</u>, with different groups <u>competing</u> for the throne. To prevent this, Elizabeth was expected to <u>marry</u> and produce an heir as <u>quickly</u> as possible.

3) Elizabeth was <u>reluctant</u> to marry — women had to <u>obey</u> their husbands, so she would <u>lose</u> her <u>power and freedom</u> if she married. Because Elizabeth <u>never married</u>, she became known as the '<u>Virgin Queen</u>'.

Comment and Analysis

Choosing a husband could create serious <u>political problems</u>. If Elizabeth chose a member of the <u>English nobility</u>, this would create <u>anger and resentment</u> among those who <u>weren't</u> chosen. But if she married a <u>European prince</u> or <u>king</u>, this could give a foreign country <u>too much</u> control over England.

The Challenges of a Female Monarch

This page will help you learn the details about the different issues Elizabeth faced when she came to power.

Knowledge and Understanding

1) Why wasn't Elizabeth expected to become queen?

2) What happened to Elizabeth in 1554?

3) Copy and complete the table below by explaining why Catholics and Protestants might have thought that Elizabeth was illegitimate. Include as much detail as you can.

	Why they might have thought that Elizabeth was illegitimate
a) Catholics	
b) Protestants	

Thinking Historically

1) Elizabeth is described on page 6 as being 'cautious'. Do you think this is a positive or negative quality for a monarch? Explain your answer.

2) Explain why each of the following was a potential challenge for Elizabeth when she became queen.
   a) her supposed illegitimacy
   b) her gender
   c) Mary I's reign

3) Copy and complete the table below by giving the possible advantages and disadvantages of Elizabeth choosing a husband and getting married. Include as much detail as you can and add as many rows as you need.

Advantages	Disadvantages

It's not easy being queen...

It's important to read the question carefully in the exam so that you only write about things that are relevant to the topic — it might help you to highlight the key words in the question.

8

Challenges at Home and From Abroad

As if the difficulties of being a female ruler weren't enough, Elizabeth also had other problems to deal with when she became queen. The economy was weak and there was a serious threat of a French invasion.

Elizabeth faced Financial Difficulties

1) Under King Edward VI, huge sums of money had been spent on wars in Scotland. Queen Mary I had also spent too much money. As a result, Elizabeth inherited enormous debts when she became queen.

2) Mary I had sold off large amounts of land owned by the Crown to cover her debts. Although this had raised money in the short term, in the longer term it reduced the monarch's income from rent.

3) The taxation system was old-fashioned and ineffective. While ordinary people faced high taxes, it had become very common for members of the nobility and gentry to pay less tax than they owed.

4) England was suffering high levels of inflation. This meant that prices were rising, while wages stayed the same or fell. The poor (see p.44) and those living in urban areas were hit hardest by inflation.

Comment and Analysis

Elizabeth was reluctant to reform the tax system and raise taxes because she feared it would upset the nobility and gentry who supported her government.

Elizabeth quickly Ended the War with France...

1) In 1557, Mary I took England to war with France. She did this to support her husband, Philip II of Spain, who was already fighting the French.

2) The war was not a success. In January 1558, the French conquered Calais, England's last remaining territory on the European mainland. This made it more difficult for the English to control the Channel, and increased the risk of a French invasion.

3) When Elizabeth became queen in November 1558, she wanted to end the war with France as quickly as possible. Peace was agreed in 1559.

Comment and Analysis

Throughout her reign, Elizabeth tried to avoid foreign wars — a policy partly influenced by England's financial weakness. She feared that raising taxes to pay for a war would be unpopular and might fuel opposition to her rule.

...but there was still a French Threat in Scotland

1) When Elizabeth became queen, Scotland was controlled by France's Catholic royal family and there were many French troops in the country. However, French rule was unpopular with many Scots.

2) In April 1558 Mary, Queen of Scots (p.16) married the heir to the French throne. As Catholics, the French royal family disliked Elizabeth (a Protestant), and wanted England to be ruled by a Catholic. Mary's marriage increased the risk the French might invade from Scotland to try to put her on the English throne.

3) In the late 1550s, Scottish Protestants, led by the preacher John Knox, rebelled against French rule. They appealed to England for support, and in 1560 English troops and ships were sent to help them.

4) The French were defeated and forced to leave Scotland. The departure of the French, combined with the death of Mary's French husband in December 1560, greatly reduced the threat of invasion.

Comment and Analysis

There were many Catholics in England who wanted to be ruled by a Catholic monarch. If the French invaded, there was a risk that the Catholics would betray Queen Elizabeth (a Protestant) and support the French.

The French Wars of Religion began in 1562 and continued until 1598. This long period of civil war between Catholics and Protestants weakened France and largely removed the threat of a French invasion for the rest of the 16th century.

Challenges at Home and From Abroad

Try these activities about the challenges Elizabeth faced due to economic problems and the French threat.

Knowledge and Understanding

1) Copy and complete the mind map below, adding details about the financial difficulties Elizabeth faced when she became queen. Include as much detail as you can.

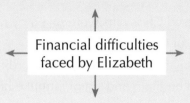

Financial difficulties faced by Elizabeth

2) Why was Elizabeth reluctant to raise taxes?

Thinking Historically

1) Copy and complete the timeline below by filling in the key events between 1557 and 1598. For each event, say whether it increased or decreased the threat from France during the 1500s.

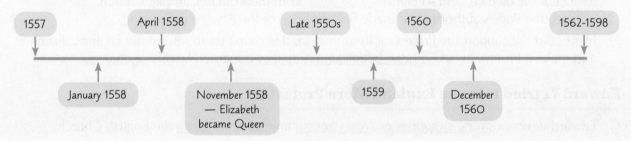

1557   April 1558   Late 1550s   1560   1562-1598

January 1558   November 1558 — Elizabeth became Queen   1559   December 1560

2) Look at the factors in the boxes below. Which one do you think was the most important factor in ending the French threat? Explain your answer.

John Knox's rebellion against French rule   The death of Mary, Queen of Scots' French husband   The French Wars of Religion

3) Why do you think the other two factors were less important? Explain your answer.

4) 'The threat of invasion from France was a more significant challenge to Elizabeth's reign than questions about her legitimacy.'
   a) Write a paragraph agreeing with the statement above.
   b) Write a paragraph disagreeing with the statement above.
   c) Write a conclusion summarising how far you agree with the statement above.

Use information from p.6 and p.8 to help with your answer.

Religious Divisions in 1558

By 1558, 30 years of dizzying religious change had created deep divisions between Catholics and Protestants.

The Protestant Reformation created religious divisions

The Protestant Reformation began in Germany in the early 16th century and gradually spread across Europe. Reformers challenged many Catholic beliefs and practices.

- The Protestant reformers believed Christians were saved by faith, not by good deeds.
- They questioned the authority of the Pope.
- They translated the Bible from Latin into languages that ordinary people could understand.
- They thought churches should be plain and simple, unlike highly decorated Catholic churches.

There had been constant Religious Changes since the 1530s

Henry VIII Broke Away from the Roman Catholic Church

1) Until the 1530s, England was a Catholic country, and most people were Catholics.

2) In the early 1530s, Henry VIII divorced his first wife, Catherine of Aragon. The Pope refused to accept the divorce, and so Henry broke away from the Roman Catholic Church. He rejected the Pope's authority and made himself head of the Church of England.

3) Henry did not support the Protestant Reformation. He didn't try to reform the English Church and make it Protestant, so Catholic beliefs and practices remained largely unchanged.

Edward VI tried to make England More Protestant

1) Edward VI was a strong supporter of Protestantism and tried to reform the English Church.

2) He made churches and church services simpler. Statues and decorations were removed from churches and priests weren't allowed to wear their elaborate Catholic vestments. A new, Protestant prayer book was issued, and church services were held in English, not Latin.

> Vestments are the robes that priests wear during church services.

Mary I Restored Catholicism and Persecuted Protestants

1) Queen Mary I was a devout Catholic. She restored the Pope as head of the English Church, removed Edward's Protestant reforms and brought back Catholic beliefs and practices.

2) Under Mary, Protestants were harshly persecuted. More than 280 people were executed for their beliefs, and hundreds more (known as Marian exiles) fled to Protestant countries in Europe.

Elizabeth I wanted Religious Stability

1) Elizabeth I had been raised as a Protestant. Although she hid her beliefs during Mary's reign to avoid being imprisoned, she was deeply religious and committed to Protestantism.

2) Elizabeth had seen the turmoil caused by Edward VI's extreme Protestant reforms and the violence of Mary I's Catholic restoration. She wanted to end the constant religious changes of the last 30 years by creating a stable and lasting religious settlement.

Religious Divisions in 1558

Now you know about the religious changes in England from the 1530s onwards, have a go at these activities.

Knowledge and Understanding

1) Where and when did the Protestant Reformation begin?

2) Summarise the ways that Protestant reformers wanted to change Catholic beliefs and practices. Include the following key words in your summary.

saved by faith   the Pope   the Bible

3) Copy and complete the table below showing how Edward VI changed religious practices in England when he became king.

Religious practices under Henry VIII	Religious practices under Edward VI
Churches were highly decorated.	a)
Priests wore elaborate vestments.	b)
A Catholic prayer book was used.	c)
Church services were held in Latin.	d)

4) In your own words, explain who the Marian exiles were.

5) Copy and complete the timeline below by adding which monarch was ruling in each period, what form of Christianity was practised, and what, if any, religious changes occurred.

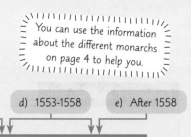
You can use the information about the different monarchs on page 4 to help you.

a) Before the 1530s   b) Early 1530s to 1547   c) 1547-1553   d) 1553-1558   e) After 1558

1530   1540   1550   1560

Thinking Historically

1) For each statement in the boxes below, write down evidence for and against it.

a) 'Henry VIII's religious changes were more extreme than Edward VI's.'

b) 'Elizabeth was more interested in religious stability than making England a Protestant country.'

c) 'The ruling monarch had absolute control over religion from the 1530s onwards.'

EXAM TIP

All these religious changes are making my head spin...

These religious divisions can be confusing, so try not to get in a muddle. Remember that Elizabeth was a Protestant, but she wanted a settlement that would appease Catholics too.

12

The Religious Settlement of 1559

After the turmoil of her predecessors' reigns, Elizabeth was determined to bring religious stability to England. In 1559, she passed her religious 'settlement', a clever compromise between Protestant and Catholic beliefs.

The Act of Supremacy gave Elizabeth Control over the Church

1) Henry VIII and Edward VI had used the title Supreme Head of the Church of England. In her Act of Supremacy (passed in 1559), Elizabeth altered this title to make herself the Supreme Governor of the English Church.

2) The Act of Supremacy required churchmen and people holding public office to swear the Oath of Supremacy. They had to recognise the Queen as Supreme Governor and promise to be loyal to her.

Comment and Analysis

The Act of Supremacy gave Elizabeth control of the English Church, without explicitly describing her as its 'Head'. This compromise satisfied those who believed a woman could not lead the Church.

3) Most parish priests took the Oath. However, all but one of the Catholic bishops refused and lost their posts. They were replaced by Protestant bishops, some of whom had been Marian exiles (see p.10).

The Act of Uniformity made Moderate Protestant Reforms

The Act of Uniformity and the Royal Injunctions, both passed in 1559, imposed moderate Protestant reforms on the English Church, but they also made some concessions to English Catholics:

Reforms

- Going to church was compulsory — there were fines for missing a church service.
- A new Book of Common Prayer was issued, which had to be used in all churches.
- All parishes had to have a copy of the Bible in English.

Concessions

- The wording of the communion service (an important Christian ceremony) was kept deliberately vague, so that it could be accepted by both Protestants and Catholics.
- Churches were allowed to keep some decorations, and priests had to wear certain Catholic vestments (robes).

Elizabeth wanted everyone in England to conform to her religious settlement. Royal commissioners were ordered to visit churches throughout the country to ensure that the Acts and Injunctions were being enforced.

Comment and Analysis

The Elizabethan religious settlement made England a Protestant country, but allowed some elements of Catholic belief and practice to continue. This clever 'middle way' was designed to satisfy the majority of the population, who held moderate religious beliefs and were willing to make some compromises for the sake of peace and stability.

The Church played an important role in English Society

1) Senior churchmen were involved in government — all bishops held a seat in the House of Lords, and the Archbishop of Canterbury was usually a member of the Privy Council.

2) Parish priests were often the most educated people in their communities, which made them respected and influential figures. As well as providing religious guidance, parish priests gave advice, helped to resolve disputes and played an important role in providing charitable support for the poor and elderly.

3) The Church helped promote national unity and obedience to the Queen. The Queen's coat of arms was often displayed in churches, and church services included prayers for the Queen and her councillors.

Queen, Government and Religion, 1558-1569

The Religious Settlement of 1559

There were lots of different parts to Elizabeth's religious settlement — each one was supposed to make sure there was religious stability in England. Try these activities to make sure you know all the important details.

Knowledge and Understanding

1) Copy and complete the diagram below by explaining why Elizabeth introduced the following changes as part of the Act of Supremacy. Give as much detail as you can.

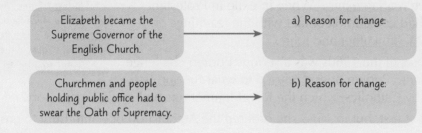

Elizabeth became the Supreme Governor of the English Church. → a) Reason for change:

Churchmen and people holding public office had to swear the Oath of Supremacy. → b) Reason for change:

2) Give three reforms introduced by the Act of Uniformity and the Royal Injunctions.

3) Write down the concessions made by the Act of Uniformity and the Royal Injunctions. For each one, explain how it helped to satisfy English Catholics.

4) Why was the religious settlement described as a 'middle way'?

5) How did Elizabeth enforce the religious settlement?

Thinking Historically

1) Copy and complete the mind map below by adding the different ways that the Church and churchmen played an important role in English government and society.

Ways that the Church and churchmen played an important role in English government and society

2) Using your completed mind map as well as information from elsewhere in the section, explain how far you agree with the following statement. 'The main purpose of Elizabeth's religious settlement was to maintain the support of the Church.'

 EXAM TIP

Sometimes the 'middle way' is the only way...

In the exam, try to be specific about the information you use. For example, instead of writing about the religious settlement generally, write about its specific parts, like the Act of Supremacy.

Challenges to the Religious Settlement

Elizabeth's religious settlement faced many challenges in the 1560s. Some were more serious than others.

The Puritans wanted to make the Church More Protestant

1) The Puritans were extreme Protestants. For them, Elizabeth's religious settlement was only a first step, and they wanted her to make further reforms to remove all traces of Catholicism from the English Church.

2) Many Puritans had been Marian exiles. While in exile in Protestant parts of Europe, some had come into contact with the teachings of leading reformers like Martin Luther and John Calvin.

3) The Vestment Controversy of the 1560s was a serious Puritan challenge to the religious settlement. Puritan priests refused to wear the surplice, a white vestment used by Catholics, which the Royal Injunctions had made compulsory.

4) Elizabeth tolerated this at first, but in 1565 she ordered the Archbishop of Canterbury to ensure that all priests wore the surplice. Those Puritans who still refused lost their jobs or were imprisoned.

> Many of the Protestant bishops appointed from 1559 supported the Puritans and were in favour of further reforms. However, the Archbishop of Canterbury, Matthew Parker, was a moderate who helped Elizabeth to uphold the 'middle way' of the religious settlement.

Some members of the Nobility continued practising Catholicism

1) A large proportion of the nobility were still Catholic. The compromises in the religious settlement won some of them around, but others refused to attend church services — they were known as recusants.

2) The Catholic nobility was influential in areas outside the south-east, especially Lancashire. They used their strong local power bases to protect Catholics and maintain their traditional religious practices.

3) These Catholic nobles posed a potential threat to the religious settlement — there was a risk that they might try to overthrow Elizabeth and restore Catholicism.

4) To minimize this threat, Elizabeth did not force the Catholic nobility to attend church services. As long as they didn't make a public show of their beliefs, they were allowed to continue practising Catholicism.

> The threat posed by the Catholic nobility became more serious when Mary, Queen of Scots, (a Catholic claimant to the English throne) arrived in England in 1568 (p.16).

France and Spain were Distracted by Domestic Difficulties

1) There was a risk that the Catholic rulers of France or Spain might try to reverse the religious settlement and replace Elizabeth with a Catholic monarch. However, neither country was really in a position to challenge the religious settlement during the 1560s.

2) The threat of a French invasion was serious in the first years of Elizabeth's reign, but faded with the start of the Wars of Religion in 1562 (see p.8).

3) In the 1560s, Spain was facing a growing revolt in the Netherlands. To prevent an alliance forming between England and the Protestant Netherlands, Spain tried to stay on good terms with Elizabeth and avoided challenging her religious settlement.

Comment and Analysis

The Catholic aspects of the settlement encouraged Catholic countries and the Pope to think that Elizabeth might eventually return to Catholicism. This helped to reduce the threat of a foreign challenge during the early years of the settlement.

The Papacy Lacked Military Support

1) The Pope had the power to excommunicate Elizabeth (expel her from the Catholic Church). This might encourage Catholic countries to invade England. It could also encourage rebellion at home by releasing Elizabeth's Catholic subjects from their duty of loyalty to her.

2) However, neither France nor Spain had the military resources to invade England, and there was no clear support for a revolt against Elizabeth at home, so the Pope didn't take any action against her in the 1560s.

Challenges to the Religious Settlement

There were several groups that opposed Elizabeth's religious settlement. You'll need to know about all these groups in the exam, so have a go at these activities to make sure you know about each one.

Knowledge and Understanding

1) Who were the Puritans? Why were many Puritans unhappy with Elizabeth's religious settlement?

2) What was the Vestment Controversy? Explain how Elizabeth responded to it.

3) How did Matthew Parker help support Elizabeth's religious settlement?

Thinking Historically

1) Copy and complete the table below about the different opponents to the religious settlement. Include as much detail as you can.

Opponent	Why were they a potential threat?	How/why was their threat reduced?
a) The Catholic nobility		
b) France and Spain		
c) The Pope		

2) 'The success of Elizabeth's religious settlement was down to luck more than anything else.' Use the information from question 1 as well as information from elsewhere in this section to structure each paragraph of an essay explaining how far you agree with this view. Each row should represent a paragraph of your essay.

Point	Evidence	Why evidence supports point
Elizabeth's religious settlement was successful because she created a compromise that satisfied both Catholics and Protestants.	Although Elizabeth was a Protestant and wanted to introduce some Protestant reforms, such as Bibles being translated into English, she also made some concessions, such as allowing churches to keep some Catholic decorations.	Elizabeth's 'middle way' was a deliberate attempt to keep both Protestants and Catholics happy. It was Elizabeth's wise decision-making, rather than luck, that meant it was successful.

Add three more rows to the table to plan three more paragraphs.

Make sure you include arguments both for and against the view expressed in the question.

Despite the settlement, things took a while to settle down...

The religious settlement aimed to create stability, but it would never be able to please everyone. It's important to remember that different groups of people had different reasons for disliking it.

Mary, Queen of Scots

Even though Elizabeth and Mary, Queen of Scots, were cousins, Elizabeth wasn't too pleased when Mary arrived in England for an unexpected visit in 1568. In fact, she was so unimpressed, she put Mary in prison...

Mary, Queen of Scots, had a Strong Claim to the English Throne

1) Mary was the only child of James V of Scotland. She was related to the Tudors through her grandmother, Margaret Tudor. Margaret was Henry VIII's sister, the wife of James IV and mother of James V (see p.4).

2) As a granddaughter of Margaret Tudor, Mary had a strong claim to the English throne. Because Mary was a Catholic, her claim was supported by many English Catholics.

3) Mary became Queen of Scotland in 1542 when she was just six days old. Her mother acted as regent (she ruled on Mary's behalf), while Mary was raised in France.

4) In 1558, when Mary was 15 years old, she married the heir to the French throne. However, her husband died suddenly in 1560, and Mary returned to Scotland.

© Mary Evans Picture Library

Comment and Analysis

Mary wanted to be named as heir to the English throne, but Elizabeth was unwilling to do this. She feared that making Mary her heir would encourage Catholic plots, both at home and abroad, to overthrow her and make Mary queen.

Mary Fled to England in 1568

1) In 1565, Mary married the Scottish nobleman Lord Darnley. The marriage was not a happy one. Darnley hated Mary's personal secretary, David Rizzio, and became convinced that the two were having an affair. In 1566, a group of Scottish nobles, accompanied by Darnley, stabbed Rizzio to death.

2) In 1567, Darnley was murdered. Many people believed that Mary and her close friend, the Earl of Bothwell, were behind the murder. Their suspicions seemed to be confirmed when Mary married Bothwell a few months later.

3) This marriage was unpopular with the Scottish nobles, who rebelled against Mary. They imprisoned her and forced her to abdicate (give up the throne) in favour of her one-year-old son, James. In 1568, Mary escaped from prison and raised an army. Her forces were defeated in battle and she fled south to England.

Some people (including Elizabeth) thought that the Scottish nobles had no right to overthrow Mary. As a result, they didn't accept her abdication, and still viewed her as the legitimate queen of Scotland.

Mary was Imprisoned, but still posed a Threat

1) Mary hoped that Elizabeth would help her regain control of Scotland. Elizabeth was not willing to do this — Mary's claim to the English throne meant that there would be a constant threat of invasion from the north if Mary regained power in Scotland.

2) Instead, Elizabeth had Mary imprisoned and set up an inquiry to investigate whether she had been involved in Darnley's murder.

3) Elizabeth didn't want the inquiry to find Mary guilty. A guilty verdict would lend support to the actions of the Scottish nobles, who had overthrown Mary, their legitimate queen.

The so-called 'Casket Letters' were presented to the inquiry. They included several letters apparently written by Mary to Bothwell, which implicated the pair in Darnley's murder. Mary's supporters insisted that the letters were forgeries, but most members of the inquiry believed they were genuine.

4) However, Elizabeth didn't want a not-guilty verdict either, because this would force her to release Mary. Once free, Mary might use her claim to the English throne to try and overthrow Elizabeth.

5) In the end, the inquiry didn't reach a verdict — this enabled Elizabeth to keep Mary in captivity. Elizabeth hoped that imprisoning Mary would prevent her becoming the centre of Catholic plots, but Mary's presence caused problems for Elizabeth throughout the next 20 years (see p.20-24).

Mary, Queen of Scots

Mary, Queen of Scots was a big problem for Elizabeth. Try these activities for a recap of the reasons why.

Knowledge and Understanding

1) Describe the key events of Mary's childhood before she returned to Scotland.

2) The flowchart below shows the key events in Mary's life between 1565 and 1568. Copy and complete the flowchart by filling in the missing information. Include as much information as you can.

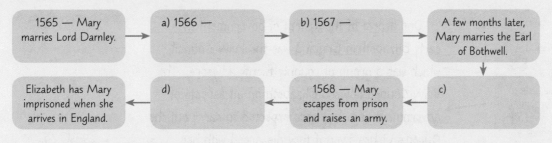

1565 — Mary marries Lord Darnley. → a) 1566 — → b) 1567 — → A few months later, Mary marries the Earl of Bothwell.

Elizabeth has Mary imprisoned when she arrives in England. ← d) ← 1568 — Mary escapes from prison and raises an army. ← c)

3) In your own words, explain why Elizabeth was unwilling to make Mary heir to the English throne.

4) What were the 'Casket Letters' and why were they important?

Thinking Historically

1) Explain how each of the factors below made Mary, Queen of Scots a threat to Elizabeth.
   a) Mary's relationship to Margaret Tudor
   b) Mary's religion
   c) The possibility of Mary regaining the Scottish throne

2) Mary was tried for Lord Darnley's murder, and either a verdict of 'guilty' or 'not guilty' at the inquiry would have caused problems for Elizabeth. Copy and complete the table, explaining what these problems were.

Verdict	Why verdict would have caused problems for Elizabeth
a) guilty	
b) not guilty	

3) What was the outcome of the inquiry? Why was this helpful for Elizabeth?

Elizabeth really wasn't a fan of uninvited guests...

When you're explaining whether or not you agree with a statement, make sure you give evidence for both sides of the argument. Don't just ignore opinions that don't match your own.

Queen, Government and Religion, 1558-1569

18

Worked Exam-Style Question

This worked answer will help you with the 4-mark question. Remember that you need to identify two clear features and give some extra information about each.

Describe two aspects of the system of government in early Elizabethan England.   [4 marks]

Identify a feature, then add some supporting information that gives a bit more detail.

One aspect of the system of government in early Elizabethan England was the Privy Council, which was a group of roughly twenty advisors. The Privy Council advised Elizabeth on all aspects of government and they were expected to carry out the Queen's wishes, even if they disagreed with her.

Another aspect of Elizabethan government was Parliament, which was made up of the nobility and gentry. Elizabeth needed Parliament's consent to pass new laws or raise taxes.

Make sure the supporting information is closely related to the aspect you've identified.

Queen, Government and Religion, 1558-1569

Exam-Style Questions

Have a go at these exam-style questions to put everything you've learnt in this section into practice. You might want to recap any pages you're not confident about before you begin.

Exam-Style Questions

1) Describe two aspects of Elizabeth's character.   [4 marks]

2) Explain why opposition to the religious settlement of 1559 didn't reach its full potential.

   You could mention:
   • Puritans
   • the Pope

   You should also use your own knowledge.   [12 marks]

3) 'When she became queen, the greatest challenge Elizabeth faced was England's financial difficulties.'

   Explain how far you agree with this statement.

   You could mention:
   • Elizabeth's legitimacy
   • Inherited debts

   You should also use your own knowledge.   [16 marks]

Challenges at Home and Abroad, 1569-1588

The Revolt of the Northern Earls

Mary, Queen of Scots, had barely been in England five minutes when she began causing trouble for Elizabeth.

The Northern Earls were unhappy for Several Reasons

1) Many northern nobles were still committed Catholics. They wanted to see the restoration of Catholicism in England under a Catholic monarch. The arrival of Mary, Queen of Scots, in 1568 (see p.16) gave them hope that Elizabeth could be replaced with Mary.

2) Elizabeth had confiscated large areas of land from the Earl of Northumberland and shared them between Northumberland's main rival in the north and a southern Protestant. Northumberland was also angry that Elizabeth had claimed all the profits from copper mines discovered on his estates.

3) Elizabeth had reduced the power of the northern nobles and increased her control in the north. In part, she did this through the Council of the North, which helped to govern the region. Under Elizabeth, the Council was controlled by southern Protestants. The northern nobles deeply resented this.

4) The northern nobles blamed Elizabeth's advisors for these policies. They believed that some privy councillors, especially William Cecil, had become too powerful. They wanted to remove these 'evil counsellors' and replace them with men who would be more sympathetic to their interests.

The Revolt of the Northern Earls broke out in November 1569

1) In 1569, the Duke of Norfolk (the wealthiest landowner in England) hatched a plan to marry Mary, Queen of Scots, and have her recognised as Elizabeth's heir. This plan was supported by Catholic nobles, including the Earls of Northumberland and Westmorland, because it meant that Elizabeth would be succeeded by a Catholic queen.

2) When the plan was uncovered, the Earls feared they would be executed for their involvement. In a desperate attempt to escape punishment, they rebelled and tried to overthrow Elizabeth.

3) In November 1569, the Earls captured Durham, where they celebrated Catholic Mass in the cathedral. They then marched south, probably making for Tutbury in Derbyshire, where Mary was imprisoned.

4) Before the rebels reached Tutbury, a large royal army forced them to retreat. Many of their troops deserted, and the two Earls fled to Scotland. Elizabeth showed the rebels little mercy. Westmorland fled abroad, but Northumberland was executed, as were at least 400 rebel troops.

The revolt was a Serious Threat to Elizabeth's rule

1) The Revolt of the Northern Earls was the most serious rebellion of Elizabeth's reign. It posed a major threat to Elizabeth's rule and showed the danger that Mary, Queen of Scots, represented as a rallying point for English Catholics.

2) News of the rebellion created widespread fear among English Protestants about Catholic plots and revenge. These fears were fuelled by memories of the harsh persecution of Protestants during the reign of Queen Mary I.

3) In 1570, Pope Pius V excommunicated Elizabeth. This was supposed to strengthen the revolt, but news of it didn't arrive until after the rebels had fled. But the excommunication did make the Catholic threat seem more serious, because it meant that Catholics no longer had to obey the Queen and were encouraged to overthrow her.

Comment and Analysis

The Revolt of the Northern Earls and the papal excommunication changed Elizabeth's attitude towards Catholics, who were now seen as potential traitors. From 1570, Elizabeth became less tolerant of recusancy and took increasingly harsh measures against English Catholics.

There was little support for the revolt among the rest of the Catholic nobility and ordinary people — when faced with a choice between Elizabeth and their religion, most Catholics chose to support the Queen. 1569-70 was the last time English Catholics tried to remove Elizabeth by force.

The Revolt of the Northern Earls

These activities will help you explain the reasons for, and impact of, the Revolt of the Northern Earls.

Knowledge and Understanding

1) Copy and complete the flowchart below by adding the missing stages in the Revolt of the Northern Earls. Include as much detail as possible.

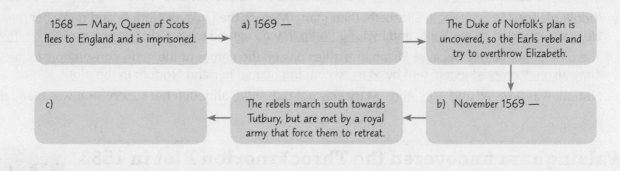

| 1568 — Mary, Queen of Scots flees to England and is imprisoned. | → | a) 1569 — | → | The Duke of Norfolk's plan is uncovered, so the Earls rebel and try to overthrow Elizabeth. |

| c) | ← | The rebels march south towards Tutbury, but are met by a royal army that force them to retreat. | ← | b) November 1569 — |

2) How did Elizabeth's attitude towards Catholics change after the Revolt of the Northern Earls?

Thinking Historically

1) Copy and complete the mind map below by adding the reasons for the Revolt of the Northern Earls in 1569. Include as much detail as possible.

Reasons for the Revolt of the Northern Earls

2) For each reason in your mind map, write down whether it was a political, religious or economic reason, or a combination of these.

3) Do you think that political, religious or economic reasons were more significant in causing the Revolt of the Northern Earls? Explain your answer.

4) 'The Pope's decision to excommunicate Elizabeth in 1570 increased the Catholic threat to Elizabeth.'
   a) Write a paragraph agreeing with the statement above.
   b) Write a paragraph disagreeing with the statement above.
   c) Write a conclusion summarising how far you agree with the statement above.

Those northern earls were revolting...

EXAM TIP

As well as knowing what happened in Elizabethan England, you'll also need to know why it happened — so be sure to learn what caused things like the Revolt of the Northern Earls.

Catholic Plots at Home

During the 1570s and 1580s, there were several Catholic plots to assassinate Elizabeth and replace her with Mary. The plots involved European conspirators and were supported by France, Spain and the Pope.

The Ridolfi Plot aimed to put Mary on the English Throne

1) Roberto di Ridolfi was an Italian banker who had played a small part in the Revolt of the Northern Earls. In 1571 he used his Catholic contacts in England and Europe to develop a plot to overthrow Elizabeth.

2) Ridolfi planned to assassinate Elizabeth, then marry Mary to the Duke of Norfolk and make her queen. He was supported by the Pope, and by King Philip II, who agreed to provide troops for a Spanish invasion.

3) The plot failed, largely because Elizabeth's allies passed the names of the main conspirators to her. They also intercepted letters sent by Mary, which implicated her and Norfolk in the plot.

4) Norfolk was arrested and executed. Mary was not punished, although her supervision was made tighter.

Walsingham uncovered the Throckmorton Plot in 1583

1) The Throckmorton Plot of 1583 aimed to assassinate Elizabeth and replace her with Mary. The conspirators planned for an invasion of England by French troops, financed by Philip II of Spain and the Pope.

2) A leading figure in the plot was Francis Throckmorton, a young Catholic man who carried messages between Mary and Catholic conspirators abroad. The plot was uncovered by Walsingham, who placed Throckmorton under surveillance for several months.

> Francis Walsingham was Elizabeth's principal secretary and spymaster. He established a large spy network in England and Europe. Walsingham intercepted the letters of Catholic conspirators and worked with an expert cryptographer to decode them. He also used double agents to infiltrate Catholic networks.

3) In response to the Throckmorton Plot, Elizabeth's closest advisors drafted the Bond of Association, which aimed to prevent any more such plots. The Bond, which was signed by the English nobility and gentry, required the signatories to execute anyone who attempted to overthrow the Queen.

The Catholic Plots posed a Real Threat to Elizabeth...

1) Mary's presence in England and her strong claim to the throne made the plots seem credible and meant that they posed a real threat to Elizabeth's rule. Many people were afraid that they would be successful.

2) As the head of the Catholic Church, the Pope could rally support for the plots. For some Catholics, obedience to the Pope was more important than obedience to Elizabeth.

3) Foreign powers, especially France and Spain, were involved in the plots, so there was a danger they would lead to a foreign invasion.

...but they had some Significant Weaknesses

1) Elizabeth was a popular ruler and the conspirators lacked public support. As the failure of the Revolt of the Northern Earls (see p.20) had shown, there was little appetite in England for a Catholic revolution.

2) Philip II was reluctant to destroy his alliance with Elizabeth. As a result, his support for the Catholic plots was half-hearted — although he promised to help the conspirators, he rarely followed through on his promises.

3) Elizabeth's informants, and later Walsingham's highly efficient spy network, ensured that the plots were uncovered before they were fully developed.

Catholic Plots at Home

More plans to overthrow Elizabeth, but still no success for the conspirators. Complete the activities below to make sure you know all the important information about each plot and why it failed.

Knowledge and Understanding

1) Copy and complete the table below by adding the relevant information about the Catholic plots to overthrow Elizabeth.

Name of plot	Who was involved?	What was their plan?	Why did it fail?
a) The Ridolfi Plot (1571)			
b) The Throckmorton Plot (1583)			

2) Make a list of similarities between the Ridolfi Plot, the Throckmorton Plot and the Revolt of the Northern Earls (see page 20).

3) What was the 'Bond of Association'? Explain how it made Elizabeth safer.

Thinking Historically

1) Look at the factors in the boxes below. Which one do you think was the most important factor in explaining why the Ridolfi Plot and Throckmorton Plot failed? Explain your answer.

> Informants and spies, including Francis Walsingham

> Elizabeth's popularity

> The plotters' use of letters

2) Why do you think the other two factors were less important? Explain your answer.

3) Copy and complete the table below by giving a piece of evidence for and against each statement.

Statement	For	Against
a) 'Philip II of Spain was an important ally to the people plotting against Elizabeth.'		
b) 'Elizabeth encouraged further plots by not punishing the conspirators involved in the Ridolfi Plot.'		
c) 'The support of the Pope was important for the Ridolfi Plot and Throckmorton Plot.'		

Don't lose the plot, just learn this page...

It's easy to think that these plots weren't a real threat because they failed, but Elizabeth treated them seriously. Think about how she responded to each plot to try to prevent any future plots.

Catholic Plots at Home

In 1586, Walsingham used his spy network to prove that Mary had supported the Babington Plot.
His evidence persuaded Elizabeth to put Mary on trial and execute her for treason.

Walsingham knew about Every Stage of the 1586 Babington Plot

1) The Babington Plot was another conspiracy involving France and Spain.
Again, the conspirators planned to assassinate Elizabeth and give the English throne
to Mary, this time with the support of a joint Franco-Spanish invasion force.

2) Anthony Babington was one of the key conspirators. He was responsible for sending information
to Mary from her supporters in England and Europe, and passing back her replies.

> Through his spy network, Walsingham followed every stage of the plot. Using a double agent,
> he managed to secretly intercept all letters sent to and from Mary, and have them decoded.
> One of Mary's letters approved plans to assassinate the Queen and free Mary from prison.

3) By August 1586, Walsingham had all the evidence he needed to break the plot.
Babington and the other conspirators were arrested, tried and executed for treason.

The Babington Plot led to the Execution of Mary, Queen of Scots

1) Mary had been implicated in Catholic plots before,
but Elizabeth had always been reluctant to take action
against her. The evidence gathered by Walsingham
finally persuaded her to put Mary on trial.

2) In October 1586, Mary was found guilty
of treason and sentenced to death.

3) After hesitating for several months, Elizabeth
eventually signed Mary's death warrant. The
execution took place on 8th February 1587.

Comment and Analysis

Because Mary was queen of Scotland, Elizabeth was
very reluctant to execute her. Elizabeth believed in the
Divine Right — that rulers were sent by God to govern
their country. Therefore, she felt she had no right to
execute a legitimate monarch. She also feared that
executing Mary would undermine her own claim to rule
by Divine Right and might fuel more plots against her.

Mary's execution Reduced the Threat from Catholics at Home...

> The execution of Mary, Queen of Scots, removed the long-standing Catholic threat to Elizabeth at home.
> English Catholics now had no-one to rally around, and they lost hope of ever overthrowing Elizabeth
> and reversing the religious settlement. There were no more major Catholic plots during Elizabeth's reign.

...but it Increased the Threat from Abroad

1) Mary's execution inflamed Catholic opposition abroad and increased the threat of a foreign invasion.

2) In 1587, relations with Spain were at a low point — the two countries were at war over the Netherlands,
and King Philip II had been preparing for an attack on England since 1585 (see p.28-32). Mary's
execution made the situation worse. Philip was now even more determined to invade.

3) There was also a danger that Mary's son, James VI of Scotland might seek
revenge for his mother's death. There were fears that he would form an
alliance with other Catholic powers in Europe in order to invade England.

Catholic Plots at Home

This is the last page about domestic plots to overthrow Elizabeth. Have a go at these activities to make sure you understand the significance of the Babington Plot and the execution of Mary, Queen of Scots.

Knowledge and Understanding

1) Who was involved in the Babington Plot?

2) Why did the Babington Plot fail?

3) Give two reasons why Elizabeth was reluctant to have Mary, Queen of Scots executed.

Thinking Historically

1) Copy and complete the mind maps below by adding the positive and negative consequences of executing Mary, Queen of Scots for the stability of Elizabeth's rule.

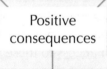

Positive consequences

Negative consequences

2) 'The Babington Plot was the most significant domestic threat faced by Elizabeth during the period 1569-1586.' Use the table below to structure each paragraph of an essay explaining how far you agree with this view. Each row should represent a paragraph of your essay.

A domestic threat is a threat from home rather than abroad.

Point	Evidence	Why evidence supports point
The Babington Plot was not a significant threat because Walsingham followed every stage of the plot from the beginning.	Walsingham used his spy network to intercept all the letters sent to and from Mary, so he knew exactly what the conspirators were plotting.	Elizabeth was never in any real danger, so the Babington Plot could not be considered a significant threat. The only reason the plot was allowed to continue as long as it did was so that Walsingham could collect enough evidence to prove the main conspirators were guilty.

Add three more rows to the table to plan three more paragraphs.

Make sure you include arguments both for and against the view expressed in the question.

You could include all the domestic threats mentioned on pages 20, 22 and 24.

The Babington Plot wasn't very well executed...

In the exam, you could be asked about any of the plots covered on the last few pages — make sure you learn about the similarities between the plots, but also their key differences.

Relations with Spain

England and Spain had tried to stay on good terms, but the rivalry between them led to growing tensions.

England and Spain were Political and Religious Rivals

1) King Philip II of Spain had been married to Queen Mary I of England, and the two countries had fought together against France in the 1550s. The war with France ended in 1559 (see p.8), but Elizabeth and Philip tried to maintain good relations with each other.

2) Spain was a great imperial power. In Europe, Philip ruled Spain, the Netherlands and parts of Italy. He also had a large empire in North and South America. In 1581, Philip became king of Portugal. This gave him control of the important Atlantic port of Lisbon, as well as Portugal's overseas empire. By the 1570s, England was starting to have ambitions for an empire of its own, and hoped to become an imperial power to rival Spain (see p.48-52).

3) Philip was a very devout Catholic and disliked the Elizabethan religious settlement of 1559. He became involved in several Catholic plots against Elizabeth in the 1570s and 1580s, although his involvement in these plots was mostly reluctant and half-hearted (see p.22).

> **Comment and Analysis**
>
> Spain's military and naval forces were much greater than England's, so Elizabeth was always reluctant to do anything that might destroy her alliance with Philip and lead to war with Spain.

There was Commercial Rivalry in the Spanish Netherlands...

English exports to Europe were vital to the English economy. Many English goods reached the European market via Dutch ports, especially Antwerp (which was in the Netherlands in the 16th century). Because Spain ruled the Netherlands, Philip could limit English access to these vital Dutch ports.

> In 1568, Spanish ships laden with gold bullion took refuge in English ports to escape bad weather. Elizabeth seized the gold for herself, which enraged Philip. In response, Philip seized English ships in Antwerp and banned English trade with the Netherlands for a time. This damaged England's economy and caused much hardship for English people.

...and in the New World

1) Trade with Spain's colonies in North and South America was very profitable, but foreigners weren't allowed to trade with them unless they had a licence. Very few Englishmen were granted licences.

2) Elizabeth encouraged privateers (men who sailed their own vessels) to trade illegally with Spanish colonies, raid Spanish ships and attack the treasure fleets carrying gold and silver from the Americas to Spain. Because the privateers were supposedly independent, Elizabeth could deny any responsibility for their activities. This helped to prevent open conflict with Philip.

3) Elizabeth received a share of the privateers' profits. Given England's financial weakness (see p.8), this was a very important source of income for her. The treasure she received from Drake in 1580 was worth more than all the rest of her income for that year put together.

© Mary Evans / INTERFOTO / Bildarchiv Hansmann

> Francis Drake was a leading privateer. He was involved in several expeditions in the New World in the late 1560s and 1570s. Between 1577 and 1580 Drake sailed around the world (see p.50). He carried out a number of raids on Spanish settlements and ships, returning with huge amounts of treasure.

> **Comment and Analysis**
>
> The Ridolfi Plot of 1571 (see p.22) damaged Elizabeth's trust in Philip and made her more willing to support the activities of English privateers.

Relations with Spain

SKILLS PRACTICE

During Elizabeth's reign, tension between England and Spain increased. Have a go at the activities on this page to help you understand what caused their relationship to deteriorate.

Knowledge and Understanding

1) Give a reason why Elizabeth wanted to maintain good relations with King Philip II of Spain at the start of her reign.

2) Explain why controlling each of the following places was beneficial for Philip II.

a) Portugal

b) The Netherlands

3) Copy and complete the table below about privateers.

	Privateers
a) What was a privateer?	
b) What three things did Elizabeth encourage the privateers to do?	
c) How did the actions of the privateers benefit Elizabeth?	
d) Why was Elizabeth more willing to support the actions of the privateers after 1571?	
e) Give the name of a leading Elizabethan privateer.	

Thinking Historically

1) Copy and complete the mind maps below, by adding the religious and economic factors that caused England's relationship with Spain to deteriorate. Use information from page 26 as well as elsewhere in the section.

Religious factors

Economic factors

2) Do you think religious factors or economic factors were more significant in causing England's relationship with Spain to deteriorate? Explain your answer, using your mind maps to help you.

EXAM TIP

The Americas — a New World of commercial rivalry...

England's relationship with Spain was a major headache for Elizabeth throughout her reign. Make sure you understand how and why the relationship between them changed over time.

War with Spain, 1585-1588

By the 1580s, the tension between England and Spain had reached boiling point. Elizabeth and Philip were still reluctant to confront one another, but in 1585 they finally went to war over the Netherlands.

Elizabeth's Support for the Dutch Rebels led to War with Spain

1) In 1581, Protestant rebels in the Netherlands declared independence from Spain and established a Dutch republic. Elizabeth gave limited financial help to the rebels, but she was reluctant to provoke Philip by getting directly involved.

2) In 1584 the rebel leader, William the Silent, was assassinated, and the Dutch revolt was in danger of being defeated. Elizabeth decided to give direct assistance to the rebels — in 1585 she signed the Treaty of Nonsuch, which placed the Netherlands under her protection and promised military assistance.

3) Several factors influenced Elizabeth's decision to sign the Treaty of Nonsuch:

Religious

Elizabeth wanted to protect Dutch Protestantism and prevent Philip forcing Catholicism on the Netherlands.

Commercial

The Netherlands' ports were essential entry points into Europe for most English exports.

Military

If the rebels were defeated, Philip might use the Netherlands as a base for an invasion of England.

Strategic

In 1584, Spain was seeking control of the French crown. If the Dutch rebels were also defeated, then Spain would control almost the entire Channel and Atlantic coasts of Europe.

Comment and Analysis

Because of her belief in the Divine Right, Elizabeth didn't want to remove Philip as ruler of the Netherlands. She just wanted to ensure freedom of worship for Dutch Protestants and protect England's military, commercial and strategic interests.

Dudley's campaigns in the Netherlands were Unsuccessful

1) Robert Dudley, Earl of Leicester, was appointed to lead the military expedition to the Netherlands. When he arrived, he accepted the position of Governor-General. This was a serious mistake — it suggested that Elizabeth had taken control of the Netherlands for herself, which risked provoking Philip even further. Elizabeth forced Dudley to resign the position immediately.

2) Dudley's campaigns of 1586-1587 were unsuccessful. He suffered several heavy defeats at the hands of the Spanish general, the Duke of Parma, and had no clear military successes. He resigned his post in 1587 and returned to England.

3) There were several reasons for the failure of the English campaigns in the Netherlands:

- Dudley wasn't a talented general.
- His officers were bitterly divided over questions of strategy.
- Dudley had a very small army compared to the number of Spanish troops.
- The English army was poorly equipped.
- Elizabeth didn't provide sufficient funds to pay the English troops.

4) English naval support for the Dutch rebels was more effective — a fleet of English ships patrolled the Dutch coastline, preventing the Spanish from landing some of their forces by sea.

War with Spain, 1585-1588

In the 1580s, England and Spain's uneasy relationship took a turn for the worse. Try your hand at these activities to help you understand what happened and why Elizabeth was prepared to protect the Netherlands.

Knowledge and Understanding

1) In your own words, explain what happened in the Netherlands in 1581.

2) What did Elizabeth agree to in the Treaty of Nonsuch?

3) Why didn't Elizabeth want to remove Philip II as ruler of the Netherlands?

4) For each of the following people, explain who they were and what their role was in the conflict in the Netherlands in the 1580s.

   a) William the Silent   b) Robert Dudley   c) The Duke of Parma

5) Copy and complete the mind map below by adding the reasons why Dudley's campaigns in the Netherlands were unsuccessful.

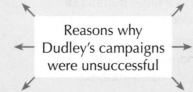

Reasons why Dudley's campaigns were unsuccessful

6) How did the English navy support the Dutch rebels?

Thinking Historically

1) In the boxes below are factors that affected Elizabeth's decision to sign the Treaty of Nonsuch. Which factor do you think had the biggest influence on her decision? Explain your answer.

   Religious factors   Commercial factors   Military factors   Strategic factors

2) Why do you think the other factors were less important? Explain your answer using information from page 28 as well as elsewhere in the section.

EXAM TIP

England and Spain — reluctant enemies...

You need to know detailed information for the four-mark question in the exam — to get full marks, you'll have to describe two features of a topic and give relevant supporting information.

Drake's Raid on Cadiz, 1587

In 1587, Francis Drake attacked the Spanish port of Cadiz. The attack, which became known as 'the singeing of the King of Spain's beard', was a major setback in Spain's preparations for the Armada.

Drake was sent to Disrupt Spanish Preparations for the Armada

- Philip saw the 1585 Treaty of Nonsuch as a declaration of war on Spain. In response, he began building a huge fleet (an Armada) that he planned to use to invade England.
- Elizabeth was aware of Philip's plans. In 1587, she sent Francis Drake, one of her most successful privateers (see p.26), to spy on Spanish preparations and attack their ships and supplies.

Drake Attacked the Spanish port of Cadiz in 1587

1) Most of the new ships for the Armada were being built in the Portuguese port of Lisbon. This deep water port was protected by strong fortifications, and Drake knew he couldn't attack it with any hope of success.

2) Instead, Drake decided to attack the port of Cadiz, which wasn't well defended. Fewer naval ships were anchored there, but the port was the centre for a large number of naval supplies, which Drake intended to seize or destroy.

3) In April 1587, Drake sailed into Cadiz harbour and began to attack the ships anchored there. He destroyed around 30 ships and seized many tonnes of supplies, including food and weapons.

4) After his successful raid on Cadiz, Drake sailed along the coast of Spain and Portugal, seizing Spanish ships and destroying supplies which were being sent to Lisbon for the Armada.

5) Drake also captured the San Filipe, a Spanish ship returning from the Americas laden with gold, spices and silk. Its valuable cargo easily covered the cost of Drake's expedition, and enabled Elizabeth to improve England's defences.

The raid on Cadiz was a Serious Setback for the Spanish Armada

1) The raid on Cadiz had a major impact on Philip's plans to invade England, delaying the Armada by more than a year.

2) Obtaining fresh supplies and weapons was very expensive and seriously strained Spain's finances.

3) During his raids, Drake captured more than 1000 tons of planks made from seasoned wood, which were needed to make the barrels used to carry food and water. As a result, the Spanish had to make their barrels from unseasoned wood, which couldn't preserve food and water very well.

> **Comment and Analysis**
>
> Drake described his raid on Cadiz as 'singeing the King of Spain's beard'. He meant that he had inflicted temporary damage on King Philip's Armada, but hadn't destroyed it entirely — it would 'grow back' in time.

4) This caused supply problems for the Armada and affected the morale of Spanish troops and sailors. Fresh water supplies were lost and many tons of food rotted as the fleet sailed to England in 1588.

Drake's Raid on Cadiz, 1587

The attack on Cadiz was a good strategic move by the English. Have a go at the activities on this page to learn the reasons for the attack and the impact it had on Spain's military preparations.

Knowledge and Understanding

1) How did Philip II respond to the Treaty of Nonsuch?

2) Why did Elizabeth send Francis Drake to the coast of Spain and Portugal in 1587?

3) Give two reasons why Drake attacked Cadiz rather than Lisbon.

4) Why did Drake describe his raid on Cadiz as 'singeing the King of Spain's beard'?

Thinking Historically

1) Copy and complete the table below by adding the consequences of each of Francis Drake's actions for the Spanish Armada.

Francis Drake's actions	Consequences for the Spanish Armada
a) **30 ships were destroyed in Cadiz harbour.**	
b) **Tonnes of food and weapons were seized or destroyed.**	
c) **Seasoned wood was stolen.**	

2) Using information from pages 26 and 30, explain why Francis Drake was important to Elizabeth's finances. Include as much detail as you can.

3) 'Francis Walsingham played a more significant role in reducing threats to Elizabeth's rule than Francis Drake.'
   a) Write a paragraph agreeing with the statement above.
   b) Write a paragraph disagreeing with the statement above.
   c) Write a conclusion summarising how far you agree with the statement above.

Turn back to p.22-24 if you need a reminder about Francis Walsingham.

EXAM TIP

I've always thought facial hair was a fire hazard...

The 'singeing of the King of Spain's beard' might sound silly, but it's a really handy phrase — it tells you a lot about the impact of Drake's raid on Philip's preparations for the Armada.

Challenges at Home and Abroad, 1569-1588

The Spanish Armada, 1588

The Spanish Armada was launched in 1588, but right from the start, things didn't go according to plan...

The Armada Planned to meet the Duke of Parma at Dunkirk

1) By the spring of 1588, the Spanish Armada was complete and Philip was ready to launch his 'Enterprise of England'. The Armada was a huge fleet of around 130 ships, manned by approximately 8000 sailors and carrying an estimated 18,000 soldiers.

2) Philip appointed the Duke of Medina Sidonia to lead the Armada. Philip respected the Duke's high social status and trusted him to obey instructions. However, the Duke had little military or naval experience, and he tried unsuccessfully to turn down the command.

3) The Spanish had thousands more soldiers stationed in the Netherlands under the leadership of the Duke of Parma. Philip's plan was for the Armada to meet Parma's army at Dunkirk. The combined forces would then sail across the Channel to England under the protection of the Armada's warships.

The Armada reached the English Channel in July 1588

1) The Armada set out in May 1588, but was delayed for several weeks by bad weather in the Bay of Biscay and by the attempts of an English fleet to intercept it.

2) In July the Spanish fleet was sighted off Cornwall and beacons (signal fires) were lit along the south coast to send the news to Elizabeth in London. English ships set sail from Plymouth to meet the Armada.

© Mary Evans Picture Library

3) The Armada sailed up the Channel in a crescent formation. This was an effective defensive strategy, which used the large, armed galleons to protect the weaker supply and troop ships.

4) The English navy carried out a few minor raids, but was unable to inflict much damage. Only two Spanish ships were lost, and these were both destroyed by accident.

The English Attacked the Spanish at Calais and Gravelines

1) Having sailed up the Channel, Medina Sidonia anchored at Calais to wait for Parma's troops. However, Parma and his men were being blockaded by Dutch ships and weren't able to reach the coast in time.

2) In the middle of the night, the English sent eight fireships (ships loaded with flammable materials and set on fire) among the anchored Spanish ships. This caused panic among the Spanish sailors, who cut their anchor cables, broke their defensive formation and headed for the open sea.

3) The Spanish ships regrouped at Gravelines, but the weather made it impossible for them to return to their defensive position at Calais. The English moved in, and the following battle lasted for many hours. Five Spanish ships were sunk, and the rest of the fleet was forced to sail away from the French coast and into the North Sea.

4) An English fleet followed the Spanish as far north as Scotland to make sure they did not regroup and return to collect Parma's army.

See p.34 for the Armada's journey back to Spain.

North Sea · Gravelines · Plymouth · Calais · Bay of Biscay · SPAIN · Lisbon

Challenges at Home and Abroad, 1569-1588

The Spanish Armada, 1588

A combination of factors meant that Philip's invasion of England didn't go according to plan. Try these activities to make sure you understand exactly what happened and why it all went wrong.

Knowledge and Understanding

1) Why did Philip appoint the Duke of Medina Sidonia to lead the Armada?
   Why was he a bad choice?

2) Describe Philip's plan to invade England. Use the key words below in your answer.

   | Duke of Parma | Dunkirk | Channel |

3) Explain how bad weather caused problems for the Spanish at each of the places below. Include as much detail as you can.
   a) The Bay of Biscay
   b) Gravelines

4) How did Dutch ships cause problems for the Armada?

Thinking Historically

1) Copy and complete the table below by explaining the outcome of each action taken by the English to stop the Armada.

Action	Outcome
a) Lighting beacons along the south coast	
b) Carrying out minor raids as the Armada sailed up the Channel	
c) Sending fireships among the Spanish ships at Calais	
d) Attacking the Spanish ships at Gravelines	
e) Following the Spanish fleet as far north as Scotland	

2) Which action do you think was the most effective at stopping the Armada? Explain your answer.

So much for King Philip's cunning plan...

In the exam, you only have a limited amount of time to answer each question. If you're spending too long on one question, write a conclusion then move on to the next question.

The Spanish Armada, 1588

The English navy had defeated the Armada, and the Spanish ships now faced a dangerous journey home.

The Armada's Journey back to Spain was a Disaster

1) Medina Sidonia decided to call off the attack on England and return to Spain by sailing round Scotland and Ireland. The Spanish sailors were unfamiliar with this very dangerous route, and they encountered several powerful Atlantic storms.

2) Many ships sank or were wrecked on the Scottish and Irish coasts, where the local inhabitants showed the survivors little mercy. Those ships that completed the journey ran short of supplies, and many men died of starvation and disease. In all, less than half the fleet and fewer than 10,000 men made it back to Spain.

Several Factors contributed to the Defeat of the Armada

English Strengths

- The English had improved their ship building, giving them several technological advantages. Spain relied on large ships which were heavy and difficult to handle, whereas the English built long, narrow ships which were faster and easier to handle. English cannons could also be reloaded much more quickly than Spanish ones.
- English tactics were more effective. Spanish ships aimed to come alongside their opponents, board their vessels and overcome the enemy in hand-to-hand fighting. The Spanish couldn't use this tactic against the English, who used their greater manoeuvrability to stay out of range. Instead of boarding the Spanish ships, the English fired broadsides (massive barrages of cannonballs) which could sink them.

Spanish Weaknesses

- Most of Spain's men lacked experience of naval warfare, whereas the English fleet was manned by experienced sailors.
- The Spanish plan to meet the Duke of Parma at Dunkirk was seriously flawed. Spain didn't control a deep water port where the Armada could anchor safely, so the ships were extremely vulnerable to an attack while it waited for Parma's troops to escape the Dutch blockade.

Luck

- The death of Spain's leading admiral, Santa Cruz, in February 1588, led to the appointment of the inexperienced Duke of Medina Sidonia to lead the Armada.
- The weather made it impossible for the Spanish fleet to return to the Channel after the battle of Gravelines, forcing it to travel into the dangerous waters off the Scottish and Irish coasts.

England's Victory Removed the threat of a Spanish Invasion

1) Philip sent two further Armadas in the 1590s, but they were both unsuccessful. Although war with Spain continued for 15 years, the Armada of 1588 was the last serious Spanish threat to Elizabeth's throne.

2) The victory of 1588 contributed to England's development as a strong naval power to rival Spain. English ships went on many voyages of discovery and established valuable trade routes, especially with India and the Far East (see p.50). By the end of Elizabeth's reign, the navy was also playing an important role in attempts to set up an English colony in North America (see p.52).

3) The English victory boosted Elizabeth's popularity and strengthened the Protestant cause — it was seen as a sign that God favoured Protestantism.

The Spanish Armada, 1588

SKILLS PRACTICE

The defeat of the Spanish Armada was not just a military success for the English — it also helped to strengthen Elizabeth's rule. This is the last page about the Armada, so make sure you understand it.

Knowledge and Understanding

1) Copy and complete the table below by adding the problems faced by the Spanish Armada at each stage of its journey back to Spain. Include as much detail as you can.

Stage of Journey	Problem(s) faced by the Armada
a) The journey round Scotland and Ireland	
b) On the Scottish and Irish coasts	
c) The rest of the journey back to Spain	

2) How many men and ships were left by the time the Armada arrived in Spain?

Thinking Historically

1) Copy and complete the mind maps below by adding reasons why the Spanish Armada was defeated. Include as much detail as you can.

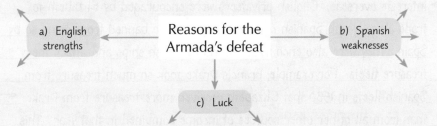

2) Copy and complete the mind map below by adding the consequences of victory over the Armada for Elizabeth and England. Include as much detail as you can.

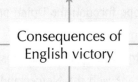

The defeat of the Armada — a great English victory...

Making essay plans can be a useful way of revising — if you can't think of much to write when you're planning an essay answer, it might mean that you need a quick recap of the topic.

Challenges at Home and Abroad, 1569-1588

Worked Exam-Style Question

The sample answer below should give you some advice for answering the 16-mark question in the exam.

'Commercial rivalry was the most important reason for the outbreak of war with Spain in 1585.'

Explain how far you agree with this statement.

You could mention:
- the Treaty of Nonsuch
- privateers

You should also use your own knowledge. [16 marks]

> The prompts in the question are only there as a guide. To get a high mark, you'll also need to include ideas of your own that go beyond the prompts.

This directly addresses the question in the first sentence.

The most important reason for the outbreak of war with Spain in 1585 was not commercial rivalry. While commercial rivalry was one of the long-term factors that contributed to growing tension between England and Spain, it was Elizabeth's involvement in the Protestant rebellion in the Netherlands that caused war to break out in 1585.

This gives a summary of the overall argument.

Commercial rivalry was an important long-term factor that caused growing tension and conflict between England and Spain, until war eventually broke out in 1585. This is because England's increasing interest in trade and colonisation in the Americas threatened Spain's economic interests overseas. English privateers were encouraged by Elizabeth to trade illegally with Spanish colonies, despite being banned from doing so by Spain. They were also encouraged to raid Spanish ships and attack their treasure fleets. For example, Francis Drake took so much treasure from Spanish fleets in 1580 that Elizabeth received more treasure from Drake than from all of her other sources of income combined in that year. This created tension because it meant that England and Spain were competing for trade opportunities and treasure.

This refers back to the question wording.

Make sure you explain how and why commercial rivalry caused tension.

Use relevant details to support your points.

Commercial rivalry was also a source of tension between England and Spain in Europe. This is because the English economy relied heavily on exporting goods to Europe through the Dutch port of Antwerp, which was under Spanish control in the 16th century. This meant that Philip was able to limit English access to Antwerp, creating tension. For example, in 1568, Philip banned English trade with the Netherlands in response to Elizabeth's decision to seize gold bullion from Spanish ships that had taken refuge in English ports. The ban on trade had a damaging effect on the English economy. This commercial rivalry was a growing source of tension that strained relations between Spain and England and made war more likely.

This shows that tension developed further because of commercial rivalry.

Make sure you link your points back to the question.

Challenges at Home and Abroad, 1569-1588

Worked Exam-Style Question

It's important to look at several factors — this shows that you've considered alternative arguments.

However, the deep religious divide between Protestant England and Catholic Spain was another long-term factor that contributed to the outbreak of war in 1585. As a devout Catholic, Philip disapproved of Elizabeth's religious settlement of 1559, which made England a Protestant country. As a result, in the 1570s and the 1580s, he supported many of the Catholic plots against Elizabeth and her religious settlement, like the Ridolfi Plot of 1571. This was directly responsible for damaging relations between England and Spain, as it made it very difficult for Elizabeth to trust Philip.

Use accurate details from your own knowledge to back up your points.

This answer compares short-term and long-term factors.

While all of these long-term factors played a key role in creating an atmosphere of tension, they did not directly provoke war. In fact, war only broke out when Elizabeth signed the Treaty of Nonsuch in 1585. Philip saw this as a declaration of war on Spain, because the treaty challenged Spain's power in Europe by promising military aid to Protestant rebels fighting against Spanish rule in the Netherlands. It also showed Philip that Elizabeth was prepared to directly intervene in Spanish affairs in order to protect Protestantism in Europe. If not for the Treaty of Nonsuch, the long-term religious and commercial tensions between the two countries might have come to nothing because both England and Spain were eager to avoid war. However, Elizabeth's decision to sign the treaty made war unavoidable.

This compares different factors and explains why one is more important than the others.

Make sure you end by clearly stating your opinion in the conclusion.

Overall, while commercial rivalry was an important factor that contributed to the build-up of tension between England and Spain, it did not directly cause war to break out in 1585. Instead, Elizabeth's decision to sign the Treaty of Nonsuch was the most important reason for the outbreak of war, because it directly triggered the opening of hostilities in 1585, building on years of tension between the two countries due to commercial rivalry and religious differences.

Exam-Style Questions

Now that you've covered everything about the challenges Elizabeth faced at home and abroad, have a go at the questions below. It might help to use information from the first section of this book for some answers.

Exam-Style Questions

1) Describe two aspects of the Ridolfi Plot in 1571.   [4 marks]

2) Explain why Elizabeth had Mary, Queen of Scots executed in 1587.

    You could mention:
    • Francis Walsingham
    • Mary's claim to the throne

    You should also use your own knowledge.   [12 marks]

3) 'Luck was the main reason why England managed to defeat the Spanish Armada.'

    Explain how far you agree with this statement.

    You could mention:
    • bad weather
    • the Duke of Medina Sidonia

    You should also use your own knowledge.   [16 marks]

Exam-Style Questions

Exam-Style Questions

4) Describe two aspects of the commercial rivalry between England and Spain between 1558 and 1588. [4 marks]

5) Explain why the northern earls revolted in 1569-1570.

You could mention:
- the Earl of Northumberland
- Mary, Queen of Scots

You should also use your own knowledge. [12 marks]

6) 'The Catholic Plots to overthrow Elizabeth failed because she was a popular ruler'.

Explain how far you agree with this statement.

You could mention:
- Francis Walsingham
- Philip II

You should also use your own knowledge. [16 marks]

Education

During Elizabeth's reign, people increasingly began to recognise the <u>importance</u> of <u>education</u>. Many <u>new schools</u> were set up and <u>more</u> people than ever learned how to <u>read</u> and <u>write</u>.

Children received a Basic Education at Home

1) Children received their early education <u>at home</u>. Most parents probably taught their children how to <u>behave correctly</u> and gave them a basic <u>religious education</u>. From the age of six, all children had to go to <u>Sunday school</u>, where they learnt things like the <u>Lord's Prayer</u>, the <u>10 Commandments</u> and the <u>Creed</u> (a basic statement of the Christian faith).

2) From a young age, boys were trained in simple <u>work skills</u>, while girls helped their mothers with <u>household activities</u>.

3) Some children from <u>noble</u> households were taught at home by a <u>private tutor</u>. Others were sent to live with another noble family and educated there.

> This kind of education was intended to teach children how to <u>behave</u> in <u>noble society</u> and give them the <u>skills</u> to be <u>successful</u> at <u>court</u>.

Petty Schools taught Reading, Writing and Maths

1) Petty schools were <u>small</u>, <u>local schools</u> that provided a <u>basic education</u>. Many petty schools were run by the local <u>parish priest</u>. Others were attached to <u>grammar schools</u>, or were set up by <u>private individuals</u>.

2) The schools taught basic <u>reading</u> and <u>writing</u>, and sometimes a little <u>maths</u>. There <u>wasn't</u> a set curriculum, although lessons usually had a strong <u>religious focus</u>. The schools <u>didn't</u> usually have any books — instead the main teaching aid was the <u>hornbook</u>, a wooden board showing the <u>alphabet</u> and the <u>Lord's Prayer</u>.

3) <u>Most</u> pupils were <u>boys</u>, although some petty schools admitted a few girls. There was <u>no fixed age</u> for pupils to start school, but they usually started at about six and stayed until they could read and write.

> Only a <u>small minority</u> of children in Elizabethan England went to <u>school</u>, but the number was <u>growing</u>. Education was increasingly <u>important</u> for many <u>careers</u>, including trade and government administration.

There was a Big Increase in the number of Grammar Schools

1) <u>Grammar schools</u> had existed for centuries, but there was a <u>big expansion</u> during Elizabeth's reign, with the foundation of around <u>100 new grammar schools</u>.

2) It was <u>very rare</u> for <u>girls</u> to go to grammar school — most pupils were <u>boys</u> from the <u>upper and middle classes</u>. Some schools offered <u>free</u> places to bright boys from <u>poorer backgrounds</u>, but <u>few</u> poor boys were able to attend because their parents needed them to <u>work</u> at home.

3) Children usually started grammar school around the age of <u>seven</u>. Lessons focused mainly on <u>Latin</u> and <u>classical literature</u> (literature from Ancient Greece and Rome), and a few schools also taught <u>Greek</u>.

> There was <u>no state education system</u> at this time. Instead, most schools were set up by <u>wealthy individuals</u>.

The number of University Students was Increasing

1) When they left grammar school, some boys went on to study at one of the two English universities, <u>Oxford</u> and <u>Cambridge</u>. The growing <u>prosperity</u> of the upper and middle classes meant that the number of university students <u>increased</u> during Elizabeth's reign.

2) University courses were conducted almost entirely in <u>Latin</u>. Students studied advanced written and spoken Latin, before moving on to study arithmetic, music, Greek, astronomy, geometry and philosophy. After completing an undergraduate degree, students might specialise in <u>law</u>, <u>theology</u> or <u>medicine</u>.

Comment and Analysis

The <u>printing press</u> had been introduced to England in the late 15th century. As printing spread, it encouraged <u>increased literacy levels</u> because it made books much <u>cheaper</u> and more <u>widely available</u>.

Education

Have a go at these activities to make sure you're clued up about Elizabethan education.

Knowledge and Understanding

1) Explain what was taught in each of the following places. Include as much detail as you can.

   a) Home   b) Sunday school   c) Petty school   d) Grammar school   e) University

2) What did pupils learn from a private tutor?

3) How were grammar schools funded in the Elizabethan period?

4) Why did some boys from poorer backgrounds turn down places at grammar schools?

Thinking Historically

1) Copy and complete the table below. For each development, explain what effect it had on education in early Elizabethan England.

Development	Effect on education
a) **Education was increasingly important for many careers.**	
b) **The upper and middle classes became more prosperous.**	
c) **The printing press was introduced to England in the late 15th century**	

2) Which of the developments in the table above do you think had the most significant effect on education in early Elizabethan England? Explain your answer.

3) For each statement in the boxes below, write down evidence for and against it.

   a) 'Religion dominated education in early Elizabethan England.'

   b) 'It was very unusual for girls to receive a good education in early Elizabethan England.'

   c) 'Poor people had very little access to education in early Elizabethan England.'

Those Elizabethans really loved their Latin...

To get a good mark in the exam, you need to support your points with facts that are accurate and relevant, so don't skip over the details when you're revising — it's all important stuff.

Sports, Pastimes and the Theatre

Some Elizabethan pastimes, including <u>tennis</u>, <u>fencing</u>, <u>football</u> and the <u>theatre</u>, are still popular today.

Hunting and Sports were an Important part of Court Life

The royal <u>court</u> was a large group of people who <u>surrounded</u> the Queen at all times. Over <u>1000 people</u> attended the court, including Elizabeth's personal servants, members of the Privy Council, nobles, ambassadors and other foreign visitors. The Queen's <u>favourite sports</u> became an important part of <u>court life</u>.

- Elizabeth and her <u>courtiers</u> often <u>hunted</u> deer and other wild animals. As well as being a form of <u>entertainment</u>, hunting was an important source of <u>food</u> for the court.
- The Queen was skilled at <u>hawking</u>, spending many hours with her trained <u>falcons</u> as they <u>hunted</u>. Training falcons was an <u>expensive</u> process, which only the <u>rich</u> could afford.
- Elizabeth's courtiers and other noblemen were expected to be skilled at <u>fencing</u> — they practised from a young age. <u>Tennis</u> and <u>bowls</u> were also becoming increasingly <u>popular</u>. These sports required <u>expensive equipment</u>, so they were only played by the <u>rich</u>.

Ordinary people had Little Time for Leisure Activities

1) Most people <u>worked</u> six days a week and went to <u>church</u> on Sundays, so they had <u>little leisure time</u>. However, there were several <u>festival days</u> in the calendar, including Midsummer's day and Ascension day. On these days, people were free to enjoy <u>sports</u>, <u>feasting</u> and other <u>pastimes</u>.
2) <u>Football</u> was a popular sport, often played between two villages. An unlimited number of players could participate, and there were <u>few rules</u>. As a result, games often descended into long and violent <u>fights</u>.
3) <u>Blood sports</u> like <u>cockfighting</u> and <u>bull- or bear-baiting</u> were also very popular. People would <u>gamble</u> on the outcome of the fights.

The Theatre became Very Popular later in Elizabeth's reign

A performance at London's Globe Theatre, which was built in 1599.

1) There were <u>no permanent theatres</u> in England at the start of Elizabeth's reign. Instead, companies of actors <u>travelled</u> around, performing in <u>village squares</u> or the <u>courtyards of inns</u>.
2) The first theatres were built in <u>London</u> in the <u>1570s</u>. They included <u>The Theatre</u> and <u>The Curtain</u>. They were usually round, <u>open-air buildings</u> with a raised stage that stretched out into the audience.
3) The theatre appealed to both <u>rich and poor</u>. Poorer audience members, known as <u>groundlings</u>, <u>stood</u> around the stage, while <u>richer</u> people sat under cover around the theatre's walls.
4) <u>Elizabeth</u> enjoyed plays and often had them performed at <u>court</u>. She supported her favourite performers and even set up an <u>acting company</u>, The Queen's Men.

Comment and Analysis

The <u>London authorities</u> and the <u>Puritans</u> opposed the theatre because they saw it as a source of <u>crime</u> and <u>immorality</u>. As a result, many theatres were built just <u>outside</u> the City of London in <u>Southwark</u>.

<u>Support</u> from the <u>elite</u> was <u>essential</u> to the development of Elizabethan theatre — acting companies relied on members of the elite to <u>fund</u> or <u>promote</u> their performances and <u>protect</u> them from opponents of the theatre. Two of the most important Elizabethan companies, <u>The Admiral's Men</u> and <u>The Lord Chamberlain's Men</u> (William <u>Shakespeare's</u> company), were supported by members of the Privy Council.

Elizabethan Society in the Age of Exploration, 1558-1588

Sports, Pastimes and the Theatre

The Elizabethans had plenty of pastimes. Some of them, like football and going to theatre, are still popular today — others, like blood sports, have (thankfully) died out. Test your knowledge with these activities.

Knowledge and Understanding

1) In your own words, explain what the royal court was.

2) Copy and complete the mind maps below by adding examples of sports enjoyed by the rich and sports enjoyed by the poor.

Sports enjoyed by the rich

Sports enjoyed by the poor

3) Why did poorer people have little time for leisure activities?

4) Copy and complete the table below about Elizabethan theatre.

	Elizabethan theatre
a) Where did actors perform before the 1570s?	
b) Where were the first theatres built?	
c) Describe what Elizabethan theatres usually looked like.	
d) Where did rich audience members sit? How was this different to poor audience members?	
e) Give the names of three Elizabethan acting companies.	

5) Why were many theatres built just outside the City of London?

6) Give two reasons why support from the elite was important for Elizabethan theatre.

I'm not sure I like the sound of Elizabethan football...

EXAM TIP

Although rich and poor people had some pastimes in common, such as the theatre, in general they spent their leisure time very differently. Think about how their experiences compared.

Elizabethan Society in the Age of Exploration, 1558-1588

44

Poverty

The growing number of people living in poverty was a major problem in Elizabethan society.

Population Growth led to Rising Prices

1) In the 16th century, England's birth rate rose and the death rate fell. This led to huge population growth — during Elizabeth's reign, the English population grew from around 3 million people to over 4 million.

2) Food production didn't keep pace with the growth in population. As a result, food prices rose and sometimes there were food shortages.

3) England also suffered several poor harvests in the 1550s and 1560s. This led to food shortages and made the problem of rising food prices even worse, causing serious hardship for the poor.

4) Prices for food and other goods rose much more quickly than wages. Standards of living fell for many workers as they struggled to afford the necessities — many were forced into poverty.

5) Because of the rapid population growth, there was growing competition for land, and so rents increased. This trend was made worse by changes in farming practices.

> In 1563, the government passed the Statute of Artificers, which set a maximum daily wage for skilled workers (e.g. butchers and carpenters). This made things even more difficult for workers, because it prevented wages from rising to match price increases.

Comment and Analysis

Henry VIII's financial problems were still having a knock-on effect early in Elizabeth's reign. Henry VIII had debased the coinage — he issued coins that were not pure gold and silver, but had cheaper metals mixed in. Businessmen believed that the coinage was worth less than before, so they put their prices up. Elizabeth's government began to tackle this problem in 1560, but it still contributed to rising prices at the start of her reign.

Developments in Agriculture left many people Unemployed

1) Traditional farming methods involved many farmers renting strips of land in large open fields. This was subsistence-level farming — each farmer only grew enough crops to supply himself and his family.

2) This kind of farming was very inefficient, and in the 16th century landowners began changing their farming techniques to try and make more money from their land. Instead of sharing open fields among many farmers, they enclosed these fields to create a few large farms.

3) These new, enclosed farms required fewer labourers, so farmers who rented land were evicted, leaving them unemployed and homeless.

4) Exporting wool to Europe was more profitable than selling grain, so many landowners stopped growing grain and began sheep farming. This fall in grain production contributed to rising food prices. It also meant that the country was more likely to suffer food shortages when there was a bad harvest.

Comment and Analysis

These enclosures of farm land forced many people to leave their villages and migrate to towns or cities in search of work. The government viewed these migrant workers as 'vagabonds'. They feared that the growth of vagabondage would encourage riots and rebellions.

Religious Changes meant there was Less Support for the Poor

1) Between 1536 and 1541, Henry VIII had closed down England's monasteries and sold off most of their land (this was called the 'dissolution of the monasteries').

2) The monasteries had performed important social functions, including providing support for many poor, ill and disabled people. The dissolution of the monasteries removed a valuable source of assistance for people in times of need.

Elizabethan Society in the Age of Exploration, 1558-1588

Poverty

Poverty was a growing problem in early Elizabethan England, and there were several different causes for this trend. Have a go at these activities to check you understand why poverty levels increased.

Knowledge and Understanding

1) Copy and complete the mind map below by giving reasons for food shortages in early Elizabethan England. Include as much detail as you can.

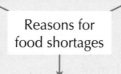

Reasons for food shortages

2) What change was introduced by the Statute of Artificers in 1563? How did it contribute to a rise in poverty?

3) What is meant by each of the following terms?
   a) debasing the coinage
   b) subsistence-level farming
   c) enclosed farms

4) What was a 'vagabond'? Why was the government worried about vagabondage? Use the key words below in your answer.

   towns and cities   migrant   riots and rebellions

Thinking Historically

1) Copy and complete the mind maps below, giving examples of how each factor led to an increase in poverty in early Elizabethan England. Include as much detail as you can.

   a) Population growth   b) Changes to agriculture   c) The actions of Henry VIII

2) Look at your mind maps from question 1. Which factor do you think had the most significant effect on poverty levels in early Elizabethan England? Explain your answer.

3) Why do you think the other two factors had a less significant effect on poverty levels in early Elizabethan England?

The enclosures closed the door to many farm labourers...

For longer essay answers, your explanation should be as clear as possible — it's really helpful to make a quick plan before you start writing to make sure that your ideas are in a logical order.

Elizabethan Society in the Age of Exploration, 1558-1588

Poverty

Elizabeth's government introduced a series of Poor Laws to try and tackle the problem of poverty.

The Government became More Involved in Poor Relief

1) Traditionally, the main source of support for the poor was charity — rich people made donations to hospitals, monasteries and other organisations that helped the poor. However, during Elizabeth's reign the problem of poverty became so bad that these charitable donations by individuals were no longer enough.

2) People began to realise that society as a whole would have to take responsibility for helping the poor, and so the government began to take action to tackle the problem of poverty.

> **Comment and Analysis**
>
> The government feared that the rising poverty levels were a serious threat to law and order. As poverty levels rose, crime rates had also increased, and the government feared that the poor might rise up in rebellion if the problem of poverty wasn't tackled.

People believed the Poor could be split into Three Categories

The Helpless Poor

Those who were unable to support themselves — including young orphans and the elderly, sick or disabled.

The Deserving Poor

People who wanted to work, but weren't able to find a job in their home town or village.

The Undeserving Poor

Beggars, criminals and people who refused to work. Also migrant workers ('vagabonds') who left their homes and travelled around looking for work.

The Poor Laws gave Help to the Helpless and Deserving Poor

1) Because voluntary donations were no longer sufficient to fund poor relief, the government began to introduce taxes to raise money for the poor.

2) The 1563 Poor Law gave magistrates the power to raise local funds for poor relief and introduced fines for people who refused to pay. However, each person was still free to decide how much they would contribute.

3) Another Poor Law in 1572 gave local officials the power to decide how much people should pay. By the end of the century there was a national system of taxation to pay for poor relief.

4) These taxes were used to provide hospitals and housing for the elderly, sick and disabled. Poor children were given apprenticeships, which usually lasted at least seven years, and local authorities were expected to provide work for the deserving poor. The Poor Law of 1576 said that poor people could be sent to prison if they refused to take work.

The Undeserving Poor were treated Harshly

Under the 1563 Poor Law, the undeserving poor could be publicly whipped. In 1572 the punishment was made even harsher — they faced whipping and having a hole bored through their right ear. Repeat offenders could be imprisoned or might even face execution.

> **Comment and Analysis**
>
> The undeserving poor were treated so harshly because they were seen as a serious threat to society. Many people believed that poor criminals and vagabonds had encouraged the Revolt of the Northern Earls in 1569 (see p.20). The harsh punishments for the undeserving poor introduced in 1572 were probably a direct response to the Revolt.

Poverty

Pages 44 and 45 should have given you a good understanding of why poverty levels rose in early Elizabethan England. These activities focus on how the government responded to the problem.

Knowledge and Understanding

1) What support was available for poor people before the Elizabethan period?

2) Write a brief definition for each of the following terms:
   a) the helpless poor
   b) the deserving poor
   c) the undeserving poor

3) Copy and complete the table below about the 1563 and 1572 Poor Laws.

Poor Law	How was money raised?	How were the undeserving poor punished?
a) 1563 Poor Law		
b) 1572 Poor Law		

4) What was the money collected from the Poor Laws of 1563 and 1572 spent on?

Thinking Historically

1) Do you agree that the Poor Laws improved life for poor people in early Elizabethan England? Explain your answer.

2) 'The threat of rebellion was the main reason why the government wanted to help the poor.' Copy and complete the table below with evidence for and against this statement.

For	Against

The Poor Laws helped some, but punished others...

Don't forget that you can make links in your answers to the important events happening at the time — many people blamed vagabonds for the Revolt of the Northern Earls, for example.

Elizabethan Society in the Age of Exploration, 1558-1588

Exploration and Discovery

Elizabeth's reign was an <u>exciting</u> time to be a sailor. Developments in <u>navigation</u> and <u>ship-building</u> were finally opening up the <u>oceans</u> and enabling explorers to discover the world <u>beyond Europe</u>.

The English were Slow to take an interest in Exploration

1) The <u>Portuguese</u> and <u>Spanish</u> were the first to explore the world beyond Europe. In the <u>1400s</u>, their fleets began to set out on <u>voyages of discovery</u> to Africa, the Americas and Asia. By the time Elizabeth became queen in 1558, both Portugal and Spain had established many <u>colonies</u> in the <u>Americas</u>.

2) However, it was only from the <u>1560s</u> that <u>English sailors</u> began to take an interest in <u>global exploration</u> and set out on their own voyages of discovery.

New Technology made Longer Journeys possible

1) Until the 15th century, most European sailors relied on <u>coastal features</u> to <u>navigate</u>. This made it <u>impossible</u> for them to cross <u>oceans</u>, where they could be out of sight of land for weeks at a time.

2) As the Portuguese and Spanish began to explore the oceans, they developed more <u>advanced navigational techniques</u>. They learnt how to navigate by the position of the <u>stars</u> or the <u>Sun</u> using a special instrument called a <u>sea astrolabe</u>.

3) During Elizabeth's reign, <u>English sailors</u> began to learn these techniques. In 1561, a key Spanish book, '<u>The Art of Navigation</u>' by <u>Martin Cortés</u>, was translated into English. This gave English sailors detailed information about how to navigate across the <u>Atlantic</u> using a <u>sea astrolabe</u>.

4) Other <u>innovations</u> helped English sailors to navigate more accurately. From the 1570s, they began using the <u>log and line</u>, which helped them to estimate their <u>speed</u> with more <u>accuracy</u>. There were also <u>improvements</u> in <u>map-making</u>, which made maps and naval charts more <u>detailed</u> and <u>reliable</u>.

> <u>Improvements</u> in <u>ship-building</u> also encouraged exploration. From the 1570s, the English began to build <u>larger, longer</u> ships. These new ships were <u>better-suited</u> to long ocean voyages because they were <u>faster, more stable</u> and <u>easier to navigate</u>. They could also carry <u>larger cargoes</u>, which made their journeys <u>more profitable</u>.

Rivalry with Spain encouraged Exploration

1) In the 1550s, English <u>international trade</u> was dominated by exports of <u>woollen cloth</u> to <u>Europe</u>. Most exports were traded through <u>Antwerp</u>, which was controlled by the <u>Spanish</u>. As <u>tensions</u> between England and Spain rose (see p.26), it became increasingly <u>difficult</u> for English merchants to <u>trade freely</u> through Antwerp.

2) This encouraged English merchants to make their international trade more <u>varied</u>. Some looked for <u>new routes</u> into <u>Europe</u>, trading with <u>German towns</u> or through the <u>Baltic</u>. Others began to look further afield, especially to the <u>Americas</u> and <u>Asia</u> (see p.50).

> Elizabeth <u>encouraged</u> the <u>development</u> of England's international trade by granting some merchants <u>monopolies</u>, which gave them <u>exclusive rights</u> to trade in a particular part of the world. E.g. in <u>1577</u> she gave a group of English merchants called the <u>Spanish Company</u> a <u>monopoly</u> on English trade with <u>Spain's colonies</u>.

3) As the <u>commercial</u> and <u>political rivalry</u> between England and Spain grew, Elizabeth realised that England needed to <u>compete</u> with Spain <u>globally</u>, not just within Europe. She encouraged English merchants to get involved in <u>long-distance trade</u> and <u>privateering</u> (see p.50), and to explore opportunities to establish English <u>colonies</u> in the <u>Americas</u> (see p.52).

Exploration and Discovery

The English hadn't really explored other continents before the 1560s, but several key changes led to a greater interest in travelling around the world. This page will help you get to grips with the facts.

Knowledge and Understanding

1) What progress had Spain and Portugal made in exploration by 1558?

2) How did English sailors navigate prior to 1561? What was the disadvantage of this method?

3) Explain how navigation improved during each of the time periods below. Include as much detail as you can.

   a) 1561

   b) From the 1570s

4) Copy and complete the mind map, adding the improvements made in ship-building from the 1570s onwards.

   ↑
   Improvements made in ship-building from the 1570s onwards
   ← →
   ↓

5) What is meant by the term 'monopoly'? Give an example of a company which had a trade monopoly during Elizabeth's reign.

Thinking Historically

1) Copy and complete the mind map below by giving ways that England's rivalry with Spain encouraged English sailors to explore the globe.

   ↖   ↗
   The role of rivalry with Spain in English exploration
   ↓

2) Do you agree that England's rivalry with Spain was the most significant reason why there was an increase in English exploration? Explain your answer.

No sat-nav? I'd have been lost in Elizabethan England...

Navigating by the Sun might not sound very advanced, but you shouldn't judge 16th-century developments by modern standards. These developments had a huge impact at the time.

Exploration and Discovery

English sailors weren't that interested in voyages of discovery at first, but once they recognised the economic opportunities on offer in the Americas and Asia, there was no stopping them.

Explorers **were Attracted** by Economic Opportunities

1) Spanish trade with its colonies in the Americas was highly profitable — their treasure ships returned to Europe full of silver and gold. The wealth of the region attracted English sailors who hoped to get rich by trading illegally with Spain's colonies and raiding Spanish settlements and treasure ships. Some also hoped to profit by establishing English colonies in the region.

2) English merchants were also keen to develop trade with Asia. Traditionally, trade in Asian luxuries like silk and spices was dominated by merchants from Venice, who kept prices very high.

3) From the 1570s, English explorers began to look for new routes to Asia which would enable them to bypass these Venetian middlemen. Some tried to find the so-called North West Passage around the top of North America, while others sailed through the Mediterranean and then went overland to India.

Francis Drake **sailed Around the World**

1) Between 1577 and 1580, Francis Drake (see p.26) sailed all the way around the world. This was only the second global circumnavigation (journey around the world) and the first by an English sailor.

2) Drake probably wasn't trying to sail around the world. It seems that he was sent by Queen Elizabeth to explore the coast of South America, looking for opportunities for English colonisation and trade. He almost certainly planned to make money on the expedition by raiding Spanish colonies and treasure ships.

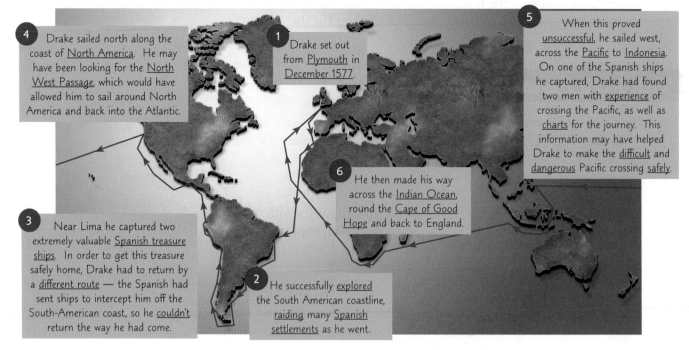

4 Drake sailed north along the coast of North America. He may have been looking for the North West Passage, which would have allowed him to sail around North America and back into the Atlantic.

1 Drake set out from Plymouth in December 1577.

5 When this proved unsuccessful, he sailed west, across the Pacific to Indonesia. On one of the Spanish ships he captured, Drake had found two men with experience of crossing the Pacific, as well as charts for the journey. This information may have helped Drake to make the difficult and dangerous Pacific crossing safely.

3 Near Lima he captured two extremely valuable Spanish treasure ships. In order to get this treasure safely home, Drake had to return by a different route — the Spanish had sent ships to intercept him off the South-American coast, so he couldn't return the way he had come.

6 He then made his way across the Indian Ocean, round the Cape of Good Hope and back to England.

2 He successfully explored the South American coastline, raiding many Spanish settlements as he went.

3) On his return to England, Drake was knighted by Queen Elizabeth aboard his ship, the Golden Hind. This royal recognition and the vast wealth that Drake brought back from the journey encouraged more English sailors to set out on long-distance journeys.

Elizabethan Society in the Age of Exploration, 1558-1588

Exploration and Discovery

SKILLS PRACTICE

Try your hand at these activities about English global exploration and the achievements of Francis Drake.

Knowledge and Understanding

1) Give two reasons why English sailors were attracted to the Americas.

2) Why were English sailors looking for new routes to Asia?

3) What routes did English sailors try to take to reach Asia?

4) The flowchart below shows the stages of Francis Drake's journey around the world from 1577 to 1580. Copy and complete the flowchart by adding the missing stages.

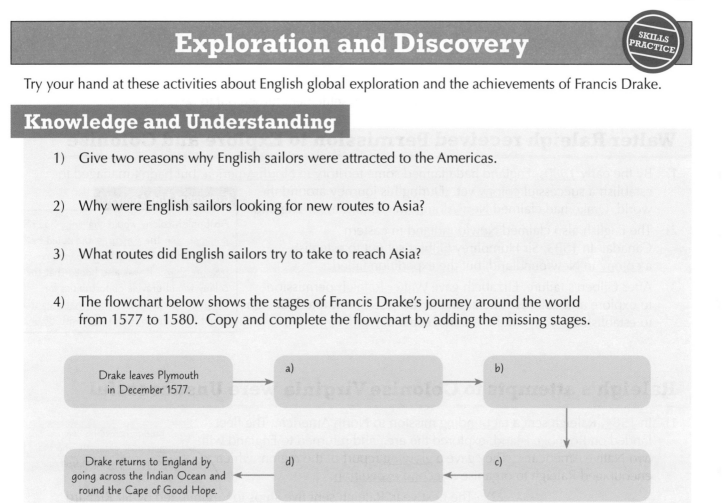

5) How were Francis Drake's achievements recognised by Queen Elizabeth? What impact did this have on other English sailors?

Thinking Historically

1) 'The search for economic opportunities was the main reason why there was an increase in English exploration and discovery.' Copy and complete the table below with evidence for and against this statement. Use information from pages 48 and 50.

For	Against

2) Which do you think was Francis Drake's biggest achievement: his expedition to the Spanish and Portuguese coast in 1587 or his circumnavigation of the world from 1577 to 1580? Explain your answer. You should use information from pages 30 and 50 to help you.

EXAM TIP

Circumnavigation — taking the roundabout route...

Don't forget to keep your answers focused on the question in the exam — it might help to link your points back to the question at the start or end of each paragraph in your essay.

Raleigh and Virginia

In the 1580s, England tried to <u>challenge</u> Spain's dominance as an imperial power by establishing a <u>colony</u> in <u>North America</u>. But creating a permanent settlement turned out to be <u>pretty tricky</u>...

Walter Raleigh received Permission to Explore and Colonise

1) By the early <u>1580s</u>, England had claimed some territory in <u>North America</u>, but <u>hadn't</u> managed to establish a successful <u>colony</u> yet. During his journey around the world, <u>Drake</u> had claimed <u>New Albion</u> (in California) for England.

2) The English also claimed <u>Newfoundland</u> in eastern Canada. In <u>1583</u>, Sir Humphrey <u>Gilbert</u> set out to establish a <u>colony</u> in Newfoundland, but the expedition <u>failed</u>.

3) After Gilbert's failure, Elizabeth gave <u>Walter Raleigh</u> permission to explore and colonise unclaimed territories. She wanted Raleigh to establish a <u>colony</u> on the Atlantic coast of <u>North America</u>.

> **Comment and Analysis**
>
> An English colony would <u>challenge</u> Spain's <u>dominance</u> in the <u>Americas</u> and could be used as a <u>base</u> for attacking Spanish <u>treasure ships</u>. It was also hoped that the colony would provide opportunities for <u>trade</u> and be a source of <u>raw materials</u> that might be useful in future <u>wars</u> with <u>Spain</u>.

Raleigh's attempts to Colonise Virginia were Unsuccessful

1) In <u>1584</u>, Raleigh sent a <u>fact-finding</u> mission to North America. The fleet landed on <u>Roanoke Island</u>, explored the area and returned to England with two Native Americans. They gave a <u>glowing</u> report of the region, which encouraged Raleigh to organise a <u>second expedition</u>.

> Raleigh named his colony Virginia after Elizabeth, who was known as the '<u>Virgin Queen</u>'.

Roanoke Island, Virginia

2) The next year, Raleigh sent five ships to <u>Virginia</u>, led by Sir Richard <u>Grenville</u>. <u>108 settlers</u> (known as <u>planters</u>) tried to establish a <u>permanent colony</u> on Roanoke, while Grenville went back to England for <u>supplies</u>.

3) When <u>Francis Drake</u> visited Roanoke in <u>1586</u>, Grenville still <u>hadn't</u> returned and the planters were running <u>low</u> on <u>supplies</u>. Most of the planters decided to <u>return to England</u> with Drake, although a small group of men were left to maintain the colony.

4) A <u>third expedition</u> reached Roanoke in <u>1587</u> and found it <u>deserted</u> — it's thought that the men who stayed behind in 1586 were <u>killed</u> by <u>local people</u>. Around <u>100 planters</u> settled on the island and began to build a colony. They were expecting <u>supplies</u> from England in <u>1588</u>, but the fleet was <u>delayed</u> by the <u>Spanish Armada</u> (see p.32-34).

5) When the supply ships finally reached Roanoke in <u>1590</u>, all the planters had <u>disappeared</u>. They were <u>never found</u>, and Roanoke soon became known as the '<u>Lost Colony</u>'.

Several Factors led to the Failure of the Roanoke Colony

Bad Timing

If the <u>supply ships</u> hadn't been <u>delayed</u> by the <u>Armada</u>, the Roanoke colony might have <u>survived</u>.

Lack of Supplies

The planters <u>didn't</u> take enough <u>supplies</u> with them and found it <u>difficult</u> to <u>grow food</u> on Roanoke. This made them more <u>vulnerable</u> to problems like the delay of the supply ships in 1588.

Poor Planning

Establishing a colony thousands of miles from England was a major <u>challenge</u>, which required detailed <u>planning</u> and <u>organisation</u>. However, initial <u>exploration</u> of Roanoke was <u>inadequate</u> and the whole project was <u>poorly organised</u>. This was largely because Raleigh's <u>funds</u> were too <u>limited</u>.

Raleigh and Virginia

SKILLS PRACTICE

As well as knowing all the key facts, it's important to understand the reasons why things happened as they did. The activities below will help you learn why Elizabeth wanted a colony and where it all went wrong.

Knowledge and Understanding

1) What territories had England already claimed in the Americas by the early 1580s?

2) Why did Elizabeth want to establish an English colony in the Americas? Include as much detail as you can.

3) Why did Walter Raleigh name his colony Virginia?

4) Copy and complete the timeline below about the attempts to colonise Virginia. Fill in all the key events between 1584 and 1590 and include as much detail as you can.

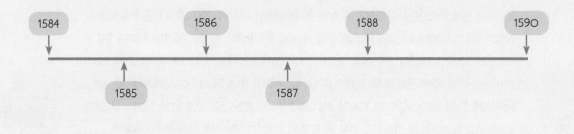

Thinking Historically

1) 'Poor planning was the most important reason for the failure of the Roanoke colony.' Use the table below to structure each paragraph of an essay explaining how far you agree with this view. Each row should represent a paragraph of your essay.

Point	Evidence	Why evidence supports point
The Roanoke colony failed because the initial exploration of the area wasn't good enough.	If the initial exploration of Roanoke Island had been more thorough, it might have picked up on issues not mentioned in the report by the Native Americans, such as the difficulty of growing food.	The initial explorations of Roanoke didn't reveal how difficult it was to grow food there. The difficulty of growing food was one of the main reasons the attempts to build a colony failed, so poor initial planning was responsible for the failure of the colony.

Add three more rows to the table to plan three more paragraphs.

Make sure you write points that agree and disagree with the statement.

As Raleigh learned, if you fail to plan, you plan to fail...

EXAM TIP

It's important to remember the order that things happened in — for example, Raleigh's attempts to colonise Virginia happened after Francis Drake's journey around the world.

Elizabethan Society in the Age of Exploration, 1558-1588

Worked Exam-Style Question

This sample answer should help you with the 12-mark question in the exam — read it carefully.

Explain why English sailors got more involved in global exploration during Elizabeth's reign.

You could mention:

- new technology
- rivalry with Spain

You should also use your own knowledge.   [12 marks]

The prompts in the question are only there as a guide. To get a high mark, you'll also need to include ideas of your own that go beyond the prompts.

> During Elizabeth's reign, English sailors took a much greater interest in global exploration than they had done previously. One of the key reasons for this was the development of new technology. Developments like the sea astrolabe, allowed sailors to navigate using the position of the stars and the Sun, so sailors no longer had to rely on coastal features to navigate and could venture into open water to cross oceans. When this became available to the English, they were able to travel across the Atlantic for the first time. Other innovations, such as the log and line, and improvements in ship-building helped to make long journeys possible, because they allowed sailors to travel more quickly and measure their speed. This meant that English sailors got more involved in global exploration because they now had the technology to explore more distant continents.
>
> Another important reason why English sailors began to explore the globe during Elizabeth's reign was because they were attracted to the opportunities to trade and make money in the Americas and Asia. English sailors knew that Spanish ships often returned to Europe full of treasure, so they were encouraged to sail to the Americas in order to trade illegally with Spain's colonies or to raid Spanish settlements and ships. English merchants were also attracted to Asia, because they hoped to make money by trading Asian luxuries without having to deal with Venetian middlemen. This meant that English sailors began looking for new routes to Asia from the 1570s onwards, for example some tried to find the North West Passage around the top of North America, while others sailed through the Mediterranean and went overland through India. Therefore, the opportunity for trade in the Americas and Asia was a key reason why the English became more involved in global exploration.
>
> The increasing tension between England and Spain in Europe also played a part in encouraging English sailors to explore new lands. In the 1550s,

The first sentence in each paragraph links back to the question.

Give specific examples to show how well you know the topic.

Including details like dates shows that you can provide accurate information.

This links the paragraph back to the question.

Elizabethan Society in the Age of Exploration, 1558-1588

Worked Exam-Style Question

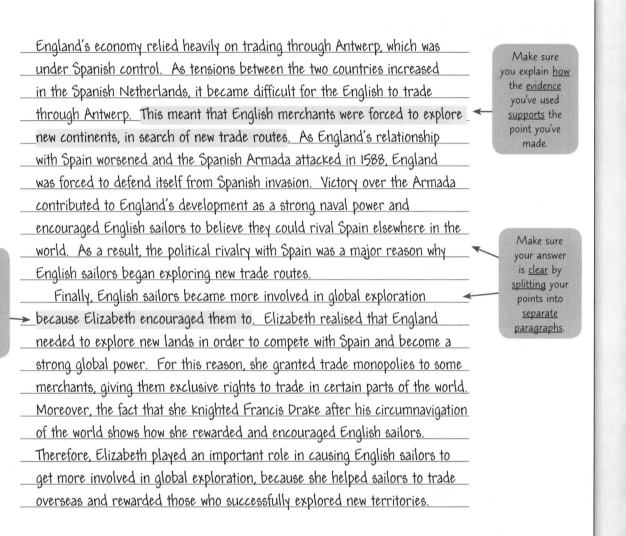

England's economy relied heavily on trading through Antwerp, which was under Spanish control. As tensions between the two countries increased in the Spanish Netherlands, it became difficult for the English to trade through Antwerp. This meant that English merchants were forced to explore new continents, in search of new trade routes. As England's relationship with Spain worsened and the Spanish Armada attacked in 1588, England was forced to defend itself from Spanish invasion. Victory over the Armada contributed to England's development as a strong naval power and encouraged English sailors to believe they could rival Spain elsewhere in the world. As a result, the political rivalry with Spain was a major reason why English sailors began exploring new trade routes.

Finally, English sailors became more involved in global exploration because Elizabeth encouraged them to. Elizabeth realised that England needed to explore new lands in order to compete with Spain and become a strong global power. For this reason, she granted trade monopolies to some merchants, giving them exclusive rights to trade in certain parts of the world. Moreover, the fact that she knighted Francis Drake after his circumnavigation of the world shows how she rewarded and encouraged English sailors. Therefore, Elizabeth played an important role in causing English sailors to get more involved in global exploration, because she helped sailors to trade overseas and rewarded those who successfully explored new territories.

Make sure you explain how the evidence you've used supports the point you've made.

Make sure your answer is clear by splitting your points into separate paragraphs.

Make sure you include factors that weren't mentioned as prompts in the question.

Exam-Style Questions

Now you know all about society and exploration in early Elizabethan England, it's time to try some practice questions. Remember to plan the 12-mark and 16-mark questions before you start writing.

Exam-Style Questions

1) Describe two aspects of university education in early Elizabethan England.   [4 marks]

2) Explain why leisure activities were different for rich people and poor people in early Elizabethan England.

   You could mention:
   - the cost of activities
   - the theatre

   You should also use your own knowledge.   [12 marks]

3) 'Francis Drake made the biggest contribution to English exploration in the early Elizabethan period.'

   Explain how far you agree with this statement.

   You could mention:
   - Drake's circumnavigation of the globe
   - the Roanoke colony

   You should also use your own knowledge.   [16 marks]

Exam-Style Questions

Exam-Style Questions

4) Describe two aspects of government policies towards the poor in early Elizabethan England. [4 marks]

5) Explain why Raleigh's attempts to colonise Virginia were unsuccessful.

You could mention:
- the Spanish Armada
- Raleigh's funding

You should also use your own knowledge. [12 marks]

6) 'Population growth was the main reason for rising levels of poverty in early Elizabethan England.'

Explain how far you agree with this statement.

You could mention:
- food shortages
- the dissolution of the monasteries

You should also use your own knowledge. [16 marks]

Answers

Marking the Activities

We've included sample answers for all the activities. When you're marking your work, remember that our answers are just a guide — a lot of activities ask you to give your own opinion, so there isn't always a 'correct answer'.

Marking the Exam-Style Questions

For each exam-style question, we've covered some key points that your answer could include.
Our answers are just examples though — answers very different to ours could also get top marks.

Most exam questions in history are level marked. This means the examiner puts your answer into one of several levels. Then they award marks based on how well your answer matches the description for that level.

To reach a higher level, you'll need to give a 'more sophisticated' answer. Exactly what 'sophisticated' means will depend on the type of question, but, generally speaking, a more sophisticated answer could include more detail, more background knowledge or make a more complex judgement.

Here's how to use levels to mark your answers:

1. Start by choosing which level your answer falls into.
   - Pick the level description that your answer matches most closely. If different parts of your answer match different level descriptions, then pick the level description that best matches your answer as a whole.
   - To do this, start at 'Level 1' and go to the next level if your answer meets all the conditions of a level. E.g. choose 'Level 3' if your answer meets all the conditions for 'Level 3' and a few of the conditions for 'Level 4'.
2. Now you need to choose a mark — look at the range of marks that are available within the level you've chosen.
   - If your answer completely matches the level description, or parts of it match the level above, then give yourself a high mark within the range of the level.
   - If your answer mostly matches the level description, but some parts of it only just match, then give yourself a mark in the middle of the range.
   - Award yourself a lower mark within the range if your answer only just meets the conditions for that level.

The 4-mark exam-style questions aren't level marked, so the mark schemes for these questions are given on the relevant page of the answers.

Level Descriptions:

12-Mark Questions:

Level 1 1-3 marks	Limited knowledge of the period is shown. The answer gives one or more simple explanations and demonstrates only a limited understanding of causation. Ideas are generally unconnected and don't follow a logical order.
Level 2 4-6 marks	Some relevant knowledge and understanding of the period is shown. The answer gives a basic analysis of the topic and demonstrates a basic understanding of causation. An attempt has been made to organise ideas in a logical way.
Level 3 7-9 marks	A good level of knowledge and understanding of the period is shown. The answer explores multiple explanations and demonstrates a good understanding of causation. It identifies some relevant connections between different points, and ideas are organised logically.
Level 4 10-12 marks	**Answers can't be awarded Level 4 if they only discuss the information suggested in the question.** Knowledge and understanding of the period is precise and detailed. The answer considers a range of explanations and demonstrates a clear understanding of causation. All ideas are organised logically. Connections between different points are identified to create a developed analysis of the topic.

16-Mark Questions:

Level 1 1-4 marks	The answer shows limited knowledge and understanding of the period. It gives a simple explanation of one or more factors relating to the topic. Ideas aren't organised with an overall argument in mind. There is no clear conclusion.
Level 2 5-8 marks	The answer shows some appropriate knowledge and understanding of the period. There is some analysis of how different factors relate to the topic. Ideas are organised with an overall argument in mind, but the conclusion isn't well supported by the answer.
Level 3 9-12 marks	The answer shows a good level of knowledge and understanding of the period, which is relevant to the question. It analyses how several different factors relate to the topic. Most ideas are organised to develop a clear argument that supports the conclusion.
Level 4 13-16 marks	**Answers can't be awarded Level 4 if they only discuss the information suggested in the question.** The answer shows an excellent level of relevant knowledge and understanding of the period. It analyses in detail how a range of factors relate to the topic. All ideas are well organised to develop a clear argument and a well-supported conclusion.

Answers

Queen, Government and Religion, 1558-1569

Page 5 — English Society and Government in 1558
Knowledge and Understanding
1 Henry VII (1485-1509), Henry VIII (1509-1547), Edward VI (1547-1553) and Mary I (1553-1558)
2 • They enforced the law.
 • They provided for the poor.
 • They ensured roads and bridges were maintained.
3 • First — Queen Elizabeth
 • Second — nobility
 • Third — gentry
 • Fourth — lawyers and merchants
 • Fifth — poor people
4 Patronage is when a monarch gives out titles and offices to the nobility or gentry.
5 a) Queen Elizabeth gained the support of the nobility and gentry by using patronage. Her decision to distribute patronage widely meant that no one felt left out, which helped to encourage loyalty to the throne.
 b) The nobility and gentry benefited from a source of income from the titles and offices that they were given.
6 a) England's population was steadily increasing.
 b) The population of towns and cities was growing rapidly.
 c) Although agriculture remained important to the economy, farming practices were changing.
 d) The export of woollen cloth to Europe was important to the economy, but merchants were starting to explore trade with the Americas and Asia.
 e) There was social inequality and the divide between rich and poor was growing.
Thinking Historically
1 a) • Privy Council — Made up of around twenty of the Queen's most trusted counsellors.
 • Parliament — Made up of members of the nobility and gentry.
 • Local government — Made up of members of the nobility and gentry who volunteered as sheriffs and Justices of the Peace.
 b) • Privy Council — It advised the Queen on all aspects of government and made sure that her wishes were carried out.
 • Parliament — The Queen needed Parliament's consent to pass new laws or raise taxes.
 • Local government — It was responsible for enforcing law and order throughout the country.
2 a) For — Elizabeth needed Parliament's consent to pass new laws or raise taxes, so her power over Parliament was limited.
 Against — Everyone in Elizabeth's government, including her closest advisors in the Privy Council, was expected to be loyal and obey her even if they disagreed with her decisions. This meant that Elizabeth had considerable power over her government.
 b) For — Parliament had the power to pass new laws and raise taxes, unlike local government officials.
 Against — Parliament could only meet when the Queen summoned it, and she only summoned it 13 times in 44 years. This restricted Parliament's power. Elizabeth relied on local government to maintain law and order throughout the country, so the power of local government was widespread.

 c) For — Elizabeth trusted the members of the Privy Council to advise her on all aspects of government, so their opinions influenced the Queen.
 Against — The Privy Council's influence was limited because its members were expected to carry out Elizabeth's wishes even if they disagreed with her.

Page 7 — The Challenges of a Female Monarch
Knowledge and Understanding
1 Elizabeth wasn't expected to become queen because she was third in line to the throne as a child, so her siblings (Edward VI and Mary I) would both rule before her.
2 In 1554, Elizabeth was accused of conspiring against Queen Mary I, who was her half-sister. She was put under house arrest for nearly a year.
3 a) Elizabeth's mother, Anne Boleyn, was married to Henry VIII. However, many Catholics thought that Henry VIII's marriage to Anne Boleyn was not valid. This is because divorce was forbidden in the Catholic Church, so they believed that Henry was still married to Catherine of Aragon when Elizabeth was born. This would have made Elizabeth illegitimate.
 b) Some Protestants questioned Elizabeth's legitimacy because Henry declared Elizabeth illegitimate in 1536 after his marriage to Anne Boleyn was dissolved, even though he later changed his mind.
Thinking Historically
1 Positive — Being cautious is a good quality for a monarch. In Elizabeth's case, it showed that she took her duty as queen seriously because she didn't want to rush into any decisions that could possibly harm the country.
 Negative — Being cautious is a negative quality for a monarch, because Elizabeth's hesitancy suggests she was a weak ruler who was unable to take decisive action.
2 a) Questions about Elizabeth's legitimacy were a challenge because they weakened her claim to the throne, and allowed supporters of Mary, Queen of Scots to declare that she had a stronger claim.
 b) Most people in the 16th century thought that a monarch should be a man and that it was unnatural for a woman to rule. This meant that many people expected Elizabeth to act as a figurehead and let her male counsellors rule for her. This was a challenge because Elizabeth had to overcome prejudice in order to rule in her own right.
 c) During Mary I's reign, there had been a lot of violence and chaos, and some people believed that this showed the dangers of having a woman as monarch, so they were unhappy when Elizabeth came to power. This was a challenge to Elizabeth because it meant that she had to overcome this prejudice as well as trying to stabilise the country following Mary's rule.
3 Advantages:
 • Choosing a husband could make Elizabeth's rule more stable because many people who didn't believe a woman could rule would assume that Elizabeth's husband would take charge of the country.
 • Marrying would allow Elizabeth to produce an heir. If she died without an heir, there would be a chance of civil war because there wouldn't be a clear successor.

Disadvantages:
- If she married, Elizabeth could lose her power and freedom because women were expected to obey their husbands.
- Choosing a husband was likely to cause political problems. If Elizabeth chose a member of the English nobility, this would anger those who weren't chosen. If she chose a European monarch, this could give a foreign country too much control over England.

Page 9 — Challenges at Home and From Abroad

Knowledge and Understanding

1
- Elizabeth faced enormous debts because England had fought a very expensive war against Scotland under Edward VI, and Mary I had overspent as well.
- The Crown's income from rent was lower than it had been because Mary I had sold a lot of the Crown's land to cover debts in the short term.
- The taxation system was old-fashioned and ineffective — the nobility and gentry often avoided paying all of the tax that they owed.
- Inflation was high, which meant that prices were rising and wages were staying the same or falling. The poor and those living in urban areas were hit hardest by inflation.

2 Elizabeth was reluctant to raise taxes because it could upset the nobility and gentry, which might lose support for her rule.

Thinking Historically

1 1557 — Mary I took England to war with France to support Phillip II of Spain, who was already fighting the French. This increased the French threat because England was now at war with France.
January 1558 — The French conquered Calais, which was England's last territory in mainland France. This increased the French threat because losing Calais made it difficult for England to control the Channel and protect itself against a French invasion from the south.
April 1558 — Mary, Queen of Scots married the heir to the French throne. This increased the risk that the French might invade from Scotland. This is because the French royal family wanted England to be ruled by a Catholic and so were more likely to invade to support Mary, Queen of Scots' claim to the throne.
November 1558 — Elizabeth became Queen. This may have increased the French threat because the French royal family wanted to replace Protestant Elizabeth with a Catholic ruler.
Late 1550s — Scottish Protestants, led by John Knox, rebelled against French rule. This reduced the threat of a French invasion of England because the French forces were preoccupied dealing with the Scottish rebellion.
1559 — Elizabeth ended Mary I's war with France and peace was agreed. This reduced the threat of invasion because England and France were no longer at war.
1560 — English troops and ships were sent to aid John Knox's rebellion in Scotland. The French were defeated in Scotland and forced to leave, which reduced the threat of invasion.
December 1560 — Mary, Queen of Scots' French husband died. This reduced the threat of a French invasion because the French royal family had less reason to put Mary, Queen of Scots on the English throne.

1562-1598 — The French Wars of Religion — French Catholics and Protestants were at war with each other. This weakened France, and decreased the threat of a French invasion.

2 You can choose any option, as long as you explain your answer. For example:
The French Wars of Religion were the most important factor in ending the French threat. The Wars of Religion were a period of civil war which lasted between 1562-1598. These wars severely weakened France, as well as diverting their attention from an invasion of England. Although Knox's rebellion and the death of Mary's French husband weakened the French threat, it was the Wars of Religion which effectively ended it altogether.

3
- John Knox's rebellion helped to diminish the French threat because it led to the French withdrawing from Scotland, making an invasion from Scotland less likely. However, it didn't end the threat completely as the French could still invade from the south — especially since England had lost Calais, which gave France more control over the Channel. Knox's rebellion was less important than the Wars of Religion because it didn't end the French threat, it just weakened France's position.
- The death of Mary's French husband in 1560 contributed to ending the French threat because the French royal family were less likely to try to put Mary on the English throne after he died. However, it was the French Wars of Religion which ultimately ended the threat because France was too weak and preoccupied to invade England.

4 a) The threat of invasion from France was a more significant challenge because the presence of French troops in Scotland made an invasion seem likely — it made it easier for the French to invade England from the north. In addition, losing Calais, and therefore control of the Channel, made England more vulnerable to a French invasion from the south. England would be especially vulnerable to invasion because Elizabeth's economic problems meant that she couldn't afford to fight a war with France. Finally, the French royal family were Catholic. This meant a French invasion could be supported by Catholics in England who wanted to replace Elizabeth with a Catholic monarch.

b) Elizabeth's possible illegitimacy was a more significant challenge because it gave Mary, Queen of Scots a claim to the throne. Both Catholics and Protestants had reasons to think that Elizabeth was illegitimate. This meant that any attempt to overthrow Elizabeth could potentially gain support from both groups, which made her possible illegitimacy a significant threat to her reign.

c) Overall, I disagree with the statement, because the threat of invasion from France was heavily reduced after 1560, while the question of Elizabeth's illegitimacy would continue to be a problem for her throughout her reign. Elizabeth could act to stop the French from invading, as she did when she sent troops to Scotland in 1560, but she could do nothing about the circumstances surrounding her birth.

Answers

Page 11 — Religious Divisions in 1558

Knowledge and Understanding

1 The Protestant Reformation began in Germany in the early 16th century.

2 Protestants believed that Christians were saved by their faith, not doing by good deeds. They didn't want the Pope to have authority over Christians, and they wanted the Bible to be written in languages that ordinary people could understand instead of Latin.

3 a) Statues and decorations were removed from churches, making them look simpler.
   b) Priests were banned from wearing elaborate vestments and had to dress more simply.
   c) A new, Protestant prayer book was issued.
   d) Church services were held in English rather than Latin.

4 Marian exiles were Protestants who fled to Europe during the reign of the Catholic Mary I to escape persecution for their beliefs.

5 a) Henry VIII — England was a Catholic country. Most people in England were Catholics.
   b) Henry VIII — Henry broke away from the Roman Catholic Church and created the Church of England. However, he didn't make many reforms to the English Church to make it Protestant — Catholic beliefs and practices continued.
   c) Edward VI — England became a Protestant country. Churches and church services became simpler — statues and decorations were removed from churches and priests were prevented from wearing elaborate vestments. Church services were held in English instead of Latin and a new Protestant prayer book was issued.
   d) Mary I — England became a Catholic country again and the Pope became the head of the English Church. Catholic beliefs and practices were brought back, undoing Edward's reforms. Many Protestants were persecuted.
   e) Elizabeth I — England became a Protestant country again, but there weren't as many extreme religious changes, because Elizabeth wanted to create religious stability.

Thinking Historically

1 a) For — Henry VIII's religious changes were more extreme because he broke away from the Catholic Church and rejected the Pope's authority. This was extreme because it went against tradition by forming a new church called the Church of England.
   Against — Edward VI's religious changes were more extreme because, unlike Henry, he reformed the English Church to make it Protestant and he removed Catholic beliefs and practices. Henry only made changes to support his divorce, whereas Edward was actually a supporter of Protestantism.
   b) For — Elizabeth knew that the religious changes of the past 30 years had caused turmoil, so she prioritised stability by creating a lasting religious settlement.
   Against — Although Elizabeth hid her beliefs to avoid being imprisoned by Mary I, she was deeply religious and strongly committed to making England a Protestant country.

   c) For — Between 1530-1558, the monarchs of England determined what religion their subjects should follow. Henry VIII created the Church of England, and Edward VI and Mary I both made extreme changes to the way that religion was practised. The people of England could face persecution if they didn't follow the monarch's orders.
   Against — Under Mary I, the Pope was the head of the English Church, so he had some control over religion in England.

Page 13 — The Religious Settlement of 1559

Knowledge and Understanding

1 a) Elizabeth became Supreme Governor to gain control over the Church of England — the title meant that she had as much power over religious practices as Henry VIII and Edward VI had when they were Supreme Heads of the Church. Being Supreme Governor instead of Supreme Head also had the advantage of satisfying those who believed that a woman couldn't be 'Head' of the Church.
   b) Making churchmen and public officials swear the Oath of Supremacy was a way of making sure they were loyal to Elizabeth. It helped her to identify the Catholic bishops who were disloyal, so that she could replace them with more loyal, Protestant bishops.

2 • They made going to church compulsory and introduced fines for missing a service.
   • They introduced a new Book of Common Prayer, which had to be used in all churches.
   • All parishes had to have a copy of the Bible in English.

3 • The communion service was vaguely worded. This meant that Catholics could interpret the service in a way that made it acceptable to them.
   • Churches were allowed some decorations and priests had to wear some Catholic vestments. This meant that some Catholic practices were preserved, which satisfied Catholics.

4 The religious settlement was described as a 'middle way' because it made England a Protestant country, but still allowed some Catholic practices to continue. It was designed to satisfy Catholics and Protestants who were willing to accept some compromises for the sake of peace and stability.

5 Elizabeth enforced the religious settlement through royal commissioners, who visited churches across the country to make sure they were obeying the Acts and Injunctions.

Thinking Historically

1 • Bishops served the government in the House of Lords.
   • The Archbishop of Canterbury usually advised the Queen as a member of her Privy Council.
   • Parish priests were influential members of the local community who gave advice and religious guidance to local people.
   • Priests provided charitable support for the poor and elderly.
   • The Queen's coat of arms was often displayed in churches, and their services included prayers for the Queen and her counsellors. This helped keep England unified and encouraged people to obey the Queen and her government.

Answers

2   Agree — Elizabeth's Act of Supremacy was used to maintain the support of the Church. This Act made Elizabeth the 'Supreme Governor' to satisfy those churchmen who didn't think a woman could be 'Head' of the Church. It also forced churchmen to pledge an Oath of Supremacy to Elizabeth, which made sure all priests and bishops were loyal to the Crown. Bishops and priests were an important tool for maintaining stability because they had a lot of influence over the local people, while senior churchmen such as bishops were involved in national government. Their support was important for promoting public loyalty to the Crown.

Disagree — The main purpose of the settlement was to maintain the support of the people, not just the Church. Elizabeth's 'middle way' was designed to keep Protestants and Catholics happy in order to encourage stability by putting an end to the turmoil and violence that religious differences had caused during the reigns of Edward VI and Mary I. Elizabeth knew that she needed to appeal to the majority of the population, and her moderate reforms helped her to achieve this.

Page 15 — Challenges to the Religious Settlement

Knowledge and Understanding

1   The Puritans were extreme Protestants. They were unhappy with Elizabeth's religious settlement because they didn't think it went far enough — they wanted to remove all the traces of Catholicism that the settlement had preserved.

2   The Vestment Controversy was a Puritan challenge to the religious settlement in the 1560s. Puritan priests refused to wear a Catholic vestment called the surplice, even though the Royal Injunctions had made it compulsory. Elizabeth was initially lenient towards the Puritans, but in 1565 she ordered all priests to wear the surplice. She dismissed or imprisoned any priests who refused.

3   Matthew Parker helped support the settlement by upholding Elizabeth's moderate 'middle way'. Although many new bishops supported the Puritans, Matthew Parker was senior to them because he was the Archbishop of Canterbury, so he had the power to enforce the settlement. For example, in 1565 he helped Elizabeth to make sure all priests were forced to wear the surplice, which the Royal Injunctions had made compulsory.

Thinking Historically

1 a)   Why were they a potential threat? — The Catholic nobility had strong influence in places like Lancashire. They had the power to protect Catholics and Catholic practices. This meant there was a risk that they could use their power to overthrow Elizabeth and restore Catholicism.

How/why was their threat reduced? — Elizabeth allowed the Catholic nobility to miss church services and practise Catholicism, as long as they didn't make a public show of their beliefs.

b)   Why were they a potential threat? — France and Spain were Catholic countries, so there was a risk that they could invade England to replace Elizabeth with a Catholic ruler. How/why was their threat reduced? — Neither country was in a position to challenge the settlement in the 1560s. The French Wars of Religion meant that France was too distracted and weak to invade England from 1562. Spain was determined to stay on good terms with England to prevent them from forming an alliance with Protestants in the Netherlands.

c)   Why were they a potential threat? — The Pope had the power to excommunicate Elizabeth and encourage a rebellion among English Catholics by releasing them from their duty of loyalty to the Queen. Excommunication could also encourage foreign invasion from Catholic countries.

How/why was their threat reduced? — France and Spain didn't have the military resources to invade England, and there was no clear support for a revolt at home. This persuaded the Pope not to take action in the 1560s. Elizabeth's settlement also had enough concessions to Catholicism to persuade the Pope that she might eventually return to Catholicism. This made the Pope more reluctant to excommunicate her.

2   Your table could include the following points:

- Point — The settlement was successful because Elizabeth made sure that the churchmen who were enforcing the religious settlement were loyal to her. Evidence — Under the Act of Supremacy in 1559, Elizabeth made churchmen and public officials swear an Oath of Supremacy. This meant they had to recognise Elizabeth as Supreme Governor of the Church and promise to be loyal to her. Most priests took the Oath, but most Catholic bishops refused. These Catholics were then replaced with Protestant bishops who were loyal to Elizabeth. Why evidence supports point — The Oath of Supremacy made it clear that churchmen had to prioritise loyalty to Elizabeth over any strong religious beliefs they had, so this was a more important factor than luck. By making sure that all the members of the Church supported her, Elizabeth ensured that the settlement didn't face as much religious opposition, which made its success more likely.

- Point — The settlement didn't face a major challenge from Catholic nobles because Elizabeth didn't force them to follow the religious settlement. Evidence — Elizabeth made concessions to Catholics by allowing Catholic nobles to miss church services for example. She also allowed them to practise Catholicism as long as they didn't display their beliefs publicly. Why evidence supports point — The threat of an uprising from Catholic nobles was reduced because of Elizabeth's ability to compromise rather than luck, which helped to make her settlement a success.

Answers

- Point — Although France and Spain were unhappy with Elizabeth's religious settlement, neither country was in a position to challenge it.
  Evidence — France had to contend with the Wars of Religion from 1562 onwards, which made them unable to invade England. Spain wanted to maintain good relations with England in the 1560s so that Elizabeth didn't support the anti-Spanish revolt that was growing in the Protestant Netherlands. As a result, Spain decided not to challenge the settlement.
  Why evidence supports point — The settlement would have been less likely to succeed if it had been challenged by a foreign invasion, and that invasion could have come if France wasn't preoccupied and Spain wasn't concerned about the revolt in the Netherlands. The fact that this challenge never materialised was not down to any of Elizabeth's actions, it was only down to luck.

Page 17 — Mary, Queen of Scots
Knowledge and Understanding
1
  - Mary became Queen of Scotland in 1542 when she was just 6 days old. She was raised in France while her mother ruled as regent.
  - In 1558, Mary married the heir to the French throne.
  - In 1560, Mary's husband died suddenly, and she returned to Scotland.
2 a) Lord Darnley becomes convinced that Mary is having an affair with her personal secretary, David Rizzio. A group of Scottish nobles, accompanied by Lord Darnley, stab Rizzio to death.
  b) Lord Darnley is murdered. It is suspected that Mary and her friend, the Earl of Bothwell, were behind his death.
  c) The Scottish nobles rebel against Mary because they disagree with her marriage to Bothwell. Mary is imprisoned and forced to abdicate her throne. Her one-year-old son, James, is made king.
  d) Mary's army is defeated in battle, and she flees to England to seek Elizabeth's help in regaining the Scottish throne.
3 Elizabeth was unwilling to make Mary heir to the throne because she was worried that this would encourage Catholic plotters to try to remove Elizabeth from power and replace her with Mary.
4 The 'Casket Letters' were letters supposedly written by Mary to Bothwell, which proved that the pair were involved in Darnley's murder. The letters were presented to the inquiry investigating Darnley's murder, so they were an important piece of evidence. Most members of the inquiry believed they were real, although Mary's supporters claimed that the letters were forgeries.

Thinking Historically
1 a) Mary was Margaret Tudor's granddaughter, which meant that she had a strong claim to the English throne. This made her a threat because she could possibly overthrow Elizabeth.
  b) Mary was Catholic, which meant that her claim to the throne may have been supported by English Catholics who wanted a Catholic queen. This increased the threat because she potentially had a lot of supporters in England.

c) If Mary regained the Scottish throne, she would have been a threat because she might be in a position to lead an invasion of England from Scotland.
2 a) A guilty verdict would have given support to the actions of the Scottish nobles who had overthrown Mary, their legitimate queen. Elizabeth viewed their actions as unacceptable and didn't want to suggest that they were right to act as they did.
  b) A not-guilty verdict would have forced Elizabeth to release Mary from prison. If Mary wasn't imprisoned, it would have been easier for her to plot against Elizabeth.
3 The inquiry didn't reach a verdict. This helped Elizabeth because it allowed her to keep Mary in prison so that there was less risk of her becoming the centre of Catholic plots. It also meant that Elizabeth didn't legitimise the Scottish nobles' rebellion.

Page 19 — Exam-Style Questions
1 Each aspect is marked separately and you can have a maximum of two marks per aspect. How to grade your answer:
  - 1 mark for describing one credible aspect of Elizabeth's character.
  - 2 marks for describing one credible aspect of Elizabeth's character and using your own knowledge to support it.
  Here are some points your answer may include:
  - Elizabeth was intelligent. This helped her to become a powerful and successful leader, despite a lack of training in government. For example, Elizabeth's religious settlement of 1559 was a clever compromise between Protestant and Catholic beliefs which helped to bring religious stability to England.
  - Elizabeth was very cautious, so she only trusted a small number of advisors. She was careful to avoid creating conflict where she could. For example, she gave herself the title of Supreme Governor of the English Church instead of Supreme Head of the Church of England. This satisfied those who believed a woman could not lead the Church.
  - Elizabeth could be indecisive. For example, Elizabeth kept Mary, Queen of Scots imprisoned for almost 20 years because Elizabeth couldn't decide how to deal with her. Elizabeth didn't want to release Mary because she knew Mary was a threat, but she also didn't want to have Mary executed because she believed in Mary's Divine Right to rule Scotland. It was only after Mary was found guilty of plotting against Elizabeth that Elizabeth finally had her executed.
  - Elizabeth was determined to rule in her own right. This prevented her from choosing a husband, as she didn't want to relinquish her power.
2 This question is level marked. You should look at the level descriptions on page 58 to help you mark your answer. Here are some points your answer may include:
  - Catholic opposition to the settlement didn't reach its full potential because Elizabeth was determined to find a 'middle way' that would satisfy moderate Catholics. She kept some Catholic traditions like elaborate vestments, and also allowed Catholic nobles to practise their faith as long as they didn't do it publicly. This gave many Catholics little reason to fully oppose the settlement.

Answers

- There was only limited opposition to the settlement from Puritans because Elizabeth punished those Puritan priests who challenged it during the Vestment Controversy. Elizabeth used support from the Protestant Archbishop of Canterbury, Matthew Parker, to ensure that any priests who refused to wear vestments after 1565 lost their jobs or were imprisoned, meaning that they were no longer in a position to challenge her settlement.
- There was a risk that the French might oppose the religious settlement because France was a Catholic country. However, opposition from France was limited because the Wars of Religion in 1562 and the defeat of the French in Scotland in 1560 meant that the French were not in a position to invade England and challenge the settlement.
- The opposition to the religious settlement from Spain, which was ruled by a Catholic, did not reach its full potential. This was because Spain wanted to stay on good terms with Elizabeth to prevent an alliance forming between England and the Protestant Netherlands, which was rebelling against Spanish rule in the 1560s.
- The Pope had the power to excommunicate Elizabeth and encourage rebellion in England, but he didn't take any action against her in the 1560s, so his opposition to the religious settlement was only limited. This was because there was no clear support for a revolt against Elizabeth in England, and the Catholic countries in Europe were either too weak or thought that it was unwise to invade England at that time. As a result, the Pope decided not to act.
- There was only limited opposition to Elizabeth's religious settlement from France, Spain and the Pope because they were encouraged by the Catholic concessions in the settlement, such as allowing priests to wear Catholic vestments. This made them believe that England might eventually become a Catholic country again, so they chose not to challenge the religious settlement.

3   This question is level marked. You should look at the level descriptions on page 58 to help you mark your answer. Here are some points your answer may include:
- Edward VI's expensive war with Scotland and Mary I's overspending meant the Crown was in enormous debts when Elizabeth took the throne. Mary I had also sold off large amounts of land owned by the Crown as a short-term solution to debt during her own reign. This meant that Elizabeth's income from Crown lands was reduced. The Crown's lack of money meant that England was vulnerable to a foreign invasion because Elizabeth didn't have the funds to finance a war.
- England had an outdated taxation system, which heavily taxed ordinary people but allowed the nobility and gentry to avoid paying the full amount that they owed. This was difficult for Elizabeth to solve because raising taxes would upset the nobility and gentry who she relied on for political support. This meant that Elizabeth's financial difficulties also threatened the stability of her reign.
- England was suffering from poverty, which was made worse by inflation. While wages stayed the same or dropped, prices were rising, which made it harder for the poor. The high level of poverty, caused by financial difficulties, was a challenge for Elizabeth because it meant that she had to choose between raising taxes for the nobility and gentry or allowing the poor to suffer.

- Some Protestants questioned Elizabeth's legitimacy because Henry VIII had declared that she was illegitimate after the execution of her mother, Anne Boleyn. While Henry later changed his mind, there was still doubt over her legitimacy. This was a challenge for Elizabeth because it meant that plots to overthrow her could gather more support, especially among Catholics.
- Elizabeth's gender was a challenge because most people believed that the monarch should be a man. The chaos of Mary I's reign only reinforced this opinion, so many people didn't support Elizabeth becoming queen because they assumed a woman couldn't rule successfully.
- Being a woman also made it difficult for Elizabeth to rule in her own right. A lot of people thought that she should marry and let her husband rule, or that she should let her male counsellors take control of government. This meant that she risked losing the support of people who thought that men would be more capable making decisions for her.
- Finding a suitable husband so she could secure the succession was a challenge for Elizabeth, since she would anger certain groups if she chose the wrong man. Choosing a foreign king or prince would have given another European country too much influence in England, whereas marriage to an English noble would have offended those nobles who weren't chosen.
- The succession was a challenging issue because Elizabeth would have faced threats to her authority regardless of what she did. Naming a legitimate claimant like Mary, Queen of Scots as her heir might have encouraged plots against Elizabeth's rule, because Mary was a Catholic so this might have encouraged Catholics to try to remove Elizabeth from power. On the other hand, failing to name an heir caused ongoing uncertainty about the succession.
- Religious divisions in England threatened Elizabeth's rule. England was in religious turmoil, as the monarchs who had come before Elizabeth had repeatedly changed the official religion. Elizabeth's religious settlement of 1559 aimed to stabilise the situation, but she faced challenges from those who didn't approve of the settlement, such as Puritans and extreme Catholics.
- Elizabeth faced threats from France and Scotland at the start of her reign. While she worked quickly to end the war with France, the marriage of Mary, Queen of Scots to the heir to the French throne in 1558 meant that Elizabeth faced the possibility of a French invasion from Scotland.

Answers

Challenges at Home and Abroad, 1569-1588

Page 21 — The Revolt of the Northern Earls
Knowledge and Understanding

1 a) The Duke of Norfolk plans to marry Mary, Queen of Scots and name her as Elizabeth's heir so that a Catholic monarch would be on the throne after Elizabeth died. The plan is supported by Catholic nobles like the Earls of Northumberland and Westmorland.

b) The Earls capture Durham and celebrate Catholic Mass in the cathedral.

c) Many of the rebel troops desert and the two Earls escape to Scotland. Although Westmorland flees abroad, Northumberland is executed, along with over 400 rebel troops.

2 After the Revolt of the Northern Earls, Elizabeth began to see Catholics as potential traitors. She became less tolerant of recusants and began to treat English Catholics more harshly.

Thinking Historically

1 • Many northern nobles were Catholics. They wanted England to be ruled by a Catholic monarch, so planned to replace Elizabeth (a Protestant) with Mary, Queen of Scots (a Catholic). (Religious)

• The Earl of Northumberland was angry at Elizabeth for taking large areas of his land and splitting them between his main rival in the north and a southern Protestant. (Political)

• Northumberland was angry that Elizabeth had claimed the profits from copper mines discovered on his estates. (Economic)

• Many northern nobles resented the fact that Elizabeth had reduced their power and increased her control in the north. They were angry because the Council of the North, which helped to govern the region, was controlled by southern Protestants. (Political/Religious)

• The northern nobles believed that some members of the Privy Council, such as William Cecil, were too powerful under Elizabeth. They wanted to remove these 'evil counsellors' and replace them with people who would be more likely to support their interests. (Political)

2 Possible answers are shown in brackets above.

3 You can choose any option, as long as you explain your answer. For example:
The Revolt of the Northern Earls happened mostly due to religious reasons, because the northern nobles' main reason for opposing Elizabeth was her religion. The original plan to make Mary, Queen of Scots Elizabeth's heir was motivated by the desire to restore a Catholic monarch to the English throne. It was only when this plan was uncovered that the Earls were forced into open revolt.

4 a) The Pope's decision to excommunicate Elizabeth increased the Catholic threat to Elizabeth because many Catholics in England no longer had to obey Elizabeth as they saw the Pope as a higher authority. Her excommunication could be seen as an invitation to overthrow her.

b) The Pope's decision to excommunicate Elizabeth had a limited effect because news of his decision didn't arrive in England until after the Revolt of the Northern Earls had failed. By this point, it was clear that there was little support in England for a revolt, even among the Catholic nobility. It was clear that most people would put their loyalty to the Queen before their religion.

c) Overall, I disagree with the statement, because the Pope's decision to excommunicate Elizabeth had little effect in reality. The Revolt of the Northern Earls was the last time that Catholics in England tried to remove Elizabeth by force, which suggests that her excommunication didn't increase the Catholic threat.

Page 23 — Catholic Plots at Home
Knowledge and Understanding

1 a) • Who was involved? — Roberto di Ridolfi, an Italian banker with Catholic contacts in Europe. The Duke of Norfolk and Mary, Queen of Scots, with the support of Philip II of Spain and the Pope.

• What was their plan? — To assassinate Elizabeth, using support from the Pope and a Spanish army provided by Philip II. The Duke of Norfolk would then marry Mary and they would rule England together.

• Why did it fail? — Elizabeth's allies passed the names of the main conspirators to her. Mary also had letters intercepted which implicated her and Norfolk.

b) • Who was involved? — Francis Throckmorton, a young Catholic man. French troops financed by Philip II of Spain, the Pope and Mary, Queen of Scots.

• What was their plan? — They planned to assassinate Elizabeth and make Mary queen. The plot was going to involve a French invasion, supported by Philip II and the Pope.

• Why did it fail? — The plot failed because Walsingham used his spy network to uncover the plot. He intercepted and decoded letters sent to and from Mary, so that he could follow every stage of the plot and keep the plotters under surveillance.

2 • All of the plots had the support of the Pope.
• All of the main conspirators were Catholic, and wanted to restore a Catholic monarch to the English throne.
• All of the plots attempted to put Mary, Queen of Scots on the throne.
• All of the plots planned to use an army to remove Elizabeth from the throne.
• All of the plots were uncovered before they could be put into action.

3 The Bond of Association was a document requiring all members of the nobility and gentry who signed it to promise to execute anyone who wanted to overthrow Elizabeth. This made her safer by giving the nobility and gentry permission to execute traitors on her behalf. It also made it clear that the punishment for treason was death, which may have deterred potential traitors.

Thinking Historically

1 You can choose any option, as long as you explain your answer. For example:
Informants and spies, such as Francis Walsingham, were the most important factor because they prevented both the Ridolfi Plot and Throckmorton Plot from succeeding. Without spies intercepting and decoding messages, these plots may not have been uncovered until it was too late. Spies and informants meant that the plots were uncovered early enough so that they never posed a real threat. The work of Elizabeth's informants also meant that she knew exactly who was involved, so she could punish the traitors.

66

2 • Although Elizabeth was a popular ruler who had a lot of public support, this popularity wasn't directly responsible for the failure of the Ridolfi Plot and Throckmorton Plot. If anything, the plots proved that Elizabeth didn't have widespread support, as several groups of extreme Catholics wanted to overthrow her.
• Although the plotters' use of letters led to them being caught, this was not the most important factor, because their tactics might have been successful if not for the work of Walsingham's spies. The letters were written in code, so they couldn't be used as evidence against the plotters unless they could be decoded — this required Walsingham to work with an expert cryptographer.

3 a) For — Philip promised troops and money to the plotters, showing that he was a valuable ally who took the plots seriously.
Against — Philip was reluctant to destroy his alliance with Elizabeth, which meant he was never fully committed to trying to overthrowing her. He ultimately broke his promises to the plotters.

b) For — Elizabeth didn't punish Mary, Queen of Scots for her role in the Ridolfi Plot, which may have encouraged her and other plotters to attempt the Throckmorton Plot.
Against — The Duke of Norfolk was executed for his involvement in the plot. This might have discouraged others from plotting to kill Elizabeth.

c) For — The Pope could encourage Catholics who were loyal to him to support the plots. He also agreed to finance the foreign invasion in the Throckmorton Plot.
Against — Although the Pope could technically rally Catholic support for the plots, there was no real appetite among English Catholics for a revolt. This meant that his support didn't have a big impact.

Page 25 — Catholic Plots at Home
Knowledge and Understanding
1 The Babington Plot involved Anthony Babington, Mary, Queen of Scots, France and Spain.
2 The plot failed because Walsingham used his spy network to follow every stage of the plot. He used a double agent to intercept letters sent to and from Mary, and then decoded the letters. Eventually, Walsingham gathered enough evidence to break the plot.
3 • Elizabeth believed in the Divine Right — she thought that rulers were sent by God to govern their countries. She felt that she had no right to execute a legitimate monarch.
• Elizabeth also worried that executing Mary would undermine her own Divine Right to rule, possibly encouraging plotters to overthrow her.

Thinking Historically
1 Positive consequences:
• Executing Mary removed a strong claimant to the throne.
• Mary had been at the centre of four Catholic plots — Catholics no longer had a figure to rally around who could legitimately replace Elizabeth as monarch.
• There were no major Catholic plots after Mary was executed.
Negative consequences:
• Mary's execution worsened relations with Spain, making Philip II more determined to invade.
• There was a danger that James VI of Scotland (Mary's son) would form an alliance with other Catholic powers in Europe and invade England to avenge his mother's death.
• Elizabeth had executed a legitimate queen who had the Divine Right to rule. This might give plotters justification to overthrow Elizabeth.
2 Your table could include the following points:
• Point — The Throckmorton Plot was the most significant domestic threat because it caused Elizabeth to take steps to protect herself from traitors.
Evidence — When the Throckmorton Plot was uncovered, Elizabeth not only had the conspirators executed, but she also introduced the Bond of Association. This required the English nobility and gentry to promise to execute anyone who attempted to overthrow the Queen.
Why evidence supports point — This suggests that the Throckmorton Plot was a significant threat to Elizabeth, because it was the only plot that made her feel so vulnerable that she passed actual legislation in response.
• Point — The Babington Plot was the most significant domestic threat because it resulted in the execution of Mary, Queen of Scots.
Evidence — Prior to the Babington Plot, Mary had been involved in three other domestic plots — the Revolt of the Northern Earls, the Ridolfi Plot and the Throckmorton Plot. After each of these plots was foiled, Elizabeth didn't punish Mary, even though she had evidence that Mary had been conspiring against her. It was only after the Babington Plot was uncovered that Elizabeth finally sentenced Mary to death.
Why evidence supports point — Mary's execution shows how significant the Babington Plot was. Even though Elizabeth was reluctant to have Mary killed because of her belief in the Divine Right, Elizabeth knew that the Babington Plot had posed a significant enough threat to justify executing Mary.

- Point — The Revolt of the Northern Earls was the most significant domestic threat because the Earls assembled an army, forcing Elizabeth to send a large royal army to stop them.
  Evidence — The revolt was the biggest show of force against Elizabeth to take place on English soil during her reign. The Earls captured Durham and gathered an army to march to Tutbury.
  Why evidence supports point — All of the other plots had the threat of invasion, but those invasions never happened. The Revolt of the Northern Earls was the only attempt to overthrow Elizabeth that posed a physical threat. Elizabeth punished the offenders harshly by executing the Earl of Northumberland and 400 rebel troops. This suggests that she saw them as a significant threat.

Page 27 — Relations with Spain
Knowledge and Understanding
1   Elizabeth wanted to maintain good relations with Spain because Spain's military and naval forces were much greater than England's, so she didn't want to risk going to war with a stronger power.
2 a) Controlling Portugal gave Philip access to the important Atlantic port of Lisbon, as well as Portugal's overseas territories.
  b) Controlling the Netherlands meant that Philip could limit English trade with Europe by blocking off Dutch ports.
3 a) A privateer was someone who sailed their own ship.
  b) Elizabeth encouraged them to trade illegally with Spanish colonies, raid Spanish ships and steal from ships carrying treasure from the Americas to Spain.
  c) Taking a share of the profits gave Elizabeth an important source of income.
  d) Philip's involvement in the Ridolfi Plot in 1571 damaged Elizabeth's trust in him, making her more willing to let privateers raid his ships and steal treasure from ships returning to Spain.
  e) Francis Drake
Thinking Historically
1   Religious factors:
- Philip was a devout Catholic, and disliked Elizabeth's 1559 religious settlement. This damaged their relationship because he wanted England to be a Catholic country.
- Philip was involved in several Catholic plots to overthrow Elizabeth, which caused her to distrust him.
- The Pope had excommunicated Elizabeth, which gave Catholic Spain a justification to be hostile towards England.
  Economic factors:
- Elizabeth seized gold from Spanish ships taking shelter in English ports in 1568, enraging Philip. He responded by seizing English ships in Antwerp and banning English trade with the Netherlands, which damaged the English economy.
- Spain refused to give licences to English traders which would have allowed them to trade with Spanish colonies. Spain's refusal denied England a very profitable trading opportunity.
- Because England couldn't trade with Spanish colonies, Elizabeth sent privateers to raid Spanish ships and steal large quantities of gold and silver.

2   You can choose either option, as long as you explain your answer. For example:
  Religious factors — When Elizabeth was excommunicated in 1570, it gave Catholic Spain greater justification to try to overthrow Elizabeth. Philip was involved in three Catholic plots between 1571 and 1586 which aimed to use Spanish armies to overthrow Elizabeth and replace her with Mary, Queen of Scots. Philip's involvement in these plots proved to Elizabeth how much of a threat Spain was, and how determined he was to overthrow her. This suggests that religious factors were the most significant reason in causing England's relationship with Spain to deteriorate, because Philip showed that he was prepared to invade England to put a Catholic on the English throne.
  Economic factors — In 1568, Philip banned England from trading with the Netherlands, which had a damaging effect on the English economy and caused hardship for people in England. In addition, Spain refused to grant licences to English traders which would have allowed them to trade with Spanish colonies. In response to this, Elizabeth encouraged privateers to raid Spanish ships and steal their cargo. Economic factors were more significant than religious factors in causing England and Spain's relationship to deteriorate because they led to concrete action from both sides, whereas the religious tension between the two countries didn't materialise into anything.

Page 29 — War with Spain, 1585-1588
Knowledge and Understanding
1   In 1581, Spain faced an uprising from Protestant rebels in the Netherlands, who declared independence and created a Dutch republic. Elizabeth aided the rebels financially.
2   Elizabeth agreed to put the Netherlands under her protection and provide military assistance to the rebels.
3   Elizabeth didn't want to remove Philip as ruler of the Netherlands because she thought he had the Divine Right to rule in the country.
4 a) William the Silent was the leader of the rebellion in the Netherlands. He was assassinated in 1584.
  b) Robert Dudley was the Earl of Leicester. He was sent to lead England's military expedition to the Netherlands. He suffered several defeats to the Duke of Parma and resigned in 1587.
  c) The Duke of Parma was the Spanish general who defeated Dudley in battle.
5 - Dudley wasn't a talented general.
  - His officers were divided over strategy.
  - Dudley's army was smaller than the Duke of Parma's.
  - The English army was poorly equipped.
  - The English army was underfunded and couldn't pay all of its troops.
6   The navy helped the Dutch rebels by patrolling the coast to prevent the Spanish from landing any more troops to fight them.

Answers

Thinking Historically

1   You can choose any option, as long as you explain your answer. For example:

Military factors had the biggest influence on Elizabeth's decision to sign the Treaty of Nonsuch. This was because, if the rebels were defeated, Philip could use the Netherlands as a base to invade England and potentially overthrow Elizabeth. The relationship between England and Spain had deteriorated by 1585, so Elizabeth knew that an invasion from Spain was a real threat and that she needed to protect herself and her country.

2   Although all of the other factors were influential, none of them were an immediate threat to Elizabeth. For example, Spain had banned trade via the Netherlands before in 1568, and although it damaged England's economy, it didn't pose a direct threat to Elizabeth's rule. Similarly, although Elizabeth wanted to support Dutch Protestants, it's unlikely she would have risked a war with Spain just to protect them — Elizabeth's 1559 religious settlement showed that she prioritised peace and stability over complete religious freedom. Finally, although Elizabeth may have been concerned by Spain increasing its territories in Europe, Spain had been growing its empire prior to the Dutch rebellion, and Elizabeth had never tried to prevent this. Her main motivation was protecting England from the threat of invasion, rather than preventing Philip from expanding his empire.

Page 31 — Drake's Raid on Cadiz, 1587

Knowledge and Understanding

1   Philip saw the treaty as a declaration of war. He began building an Armada so he could invade England.

2   Drake was sent to spy on Spain's preparations for the Armada, and to attack Spanish ships and supplies.

3   • Cadiz wasn't as well defended as Lisbon, so Drake had a better chance of success.

     • The port was the centre for a large number of naval supplies, and their destruction would be a massive setback for the Spanish invasion.

4   Drake described the raid as 'singeing the King of Spain's beard' because he thought he had inflicted temporary damage on the Spanish Armada, but hadn't completely destroyed it — it would eventually 'grow back' like a beard.

Thinking Historically

1 a)   The Spanish Armada lost ships that would have to be rebuilt. This delayed the Armada by over a year.

   b)   Spain had to replace the supplies, which was very expensive and strained its finances.

   c)   The Spanish had to make food and water barrels from unseasoned wood. Food and water wasn't preserved very well, which meant fresh water was lost and food rotted on the way to England. This damaged the morale of the Spanish forces.

2   Drake boosted Elizabeth's finances. The stolen treasure he gave to England in 1580 was more than the rest of its income for the year put together. This helped to keep the country financially stable. Drake's capture of the *San Filipe* covered the cost of his expedition to the Spanish coast and provided money for Elizabeth to improve England's defences before the Armada arrived.

3 a)   Francis Walsingham was instrumental in preventing a number of plots to overthrow Elizabeth. The spy network he established protected Elizabeth against plots from all over Europe. He intercepted letters from conspirators and decoded them and infiltrated plots with double agents, preventing Elizabeth from being overthrown by stopping the plotters before they could carry out their plans. Walsingham also implicated Mary, Queen of Scots in multiple plots, which led to her eventual execution. This removed a major threat to Elizabeth's rule, as Catholic conspirators no longer had an alternative monarch to rally around. Without Walsingham, the likelihood of Elizabeth being overthrown would have been far higher, and her reign may have ended long before the Armada set sail.

   b)   Francis Drake's raid on Cadiz delayed the Armada and provided Elizabeth with intelligence on Spain's plans, which strengthened England against a Spanish invasion. The Spanish invasion was delayed by more than a year because of the damage done at Cadiz, which gave Elizabeth extra time to take measures to protect England. Drake also provided Elizabeth with valuable treasure, which allowed her to raise money to improve England's defences. Drake captured over 1000 tons of seasoned wood during his raids, which meant that the Spanish had to use unseasoned wood to make barrels to preserve food and fresh water. This caused food to rot during the journey to England, which damaged the Armada's morale. The Spanish Armada was one of the most significant threats to Elizabeth's rule, and Drake's expedition helped to lessen this threat.

   c)   You can choose any option, as long as you explain your answer. For example:

Walsingham played a more significant role in reducing threats from foreign invasion. Walsingham's actions directly protected the Queen from assassination attempts. Although Drake's actions delayed the Armada, he didn't defeat it entirely, so Drake played a less significant role in reducing threats to Elizabeth's rule.

Page 33 — The Spanish Armada, 1588

Knowledge and Understanding

1   Philip appointed the Duke of Medina Sidonia because he respected his high social status and trusted him to obey instructions. He was a bad choice because he had little naval or military experience and he didn't want the role.

2   Philip planned for the Armada to sail to Dunkirk to meet thousands of soldiers led by the Duke of Parma. This army would then sail across the Channel to England, protected by the Armada's warships.

3 a)   Bad weather in the Bay of Biscay meant the Armada was delayed by several weeks.

   b)   The bad weather at Gravelines made it impossible for the Armada to return to its stronger defensive position at Calais. This made it more vulnerable to English attack.

4   The Dutch caused problems for the Armada by blockading the Duke of Parma's forces, which prevented them from reaching the coast to meet the invasion fleet at Calais.

Answers

Thinking Historically

1 a) Lighting beacons along the south coast meant that news of the invasion reached Elizabeth in London quickly, warning her about the Armada's arrival in the Channel.

b) The raids caused little damage. Two Spanish ships were lost, but they were both destroyed by accident.

c) The fireships caused panic among the Spanish sailors, making them cut their anchor cables, break formation and head to the open sea.

d) The attack at Gravelines led to five Spanish ships being destroyed, and the rest of the Armada was forced to flee to the North Sea.

e) Following the Armada to Scotland meant that it couldn't regroup and prevented it from returning to meet with Parma's troops.

2 You can choose any option, as long as you explain your answer. For example:

Sending fireships among the Spanish ships was the most effective action because it gave the English a way to defeat the Armada in battle. The panic caused by the fireships led to the Spanish heading to open water, so they couldn't return to their defensive position at Calais. This made the Spanish ships more vulnerable to attack.

Page 35 — The Spanish Armada, 1588

Knowledge and Understanding

1 a) Powerful Atlantic storms made it difficult for the sailors to navigate a route they were already unfamiliar with. Some of the ships sank.

b) Many ships were wrecked on the Scottish and Irish coasts. The local inhabitants showed the survivors little mercy.

c) There was a lack of supplies, causing many men to die of starvation. Some also died of disease.

2 Fewer than 10,000 men were left and less than half the fleet of ships (fewer than 65).

Thinking Historically

1 a) • English ship-building had improved. Their long, narrow ships were a lot faster and easier to handle than Spain's larger ships. This meant they could stay out of range of Spanish ships, which prevented them from being boarded. English cannons reloaded quicker, which allowed them to do more damage to Spanish ships in less time.

• English tactics were more effective. The English stayed out of range so they weren't boarded, and fired broadsides to sink Spanish ships instead of relying on hand-to-hand combat.

b) • The Spanish sailors were less experienced than the English sailors. This meant they went into battle against an English fleet that was more used to naval warfare.

• Spain didn't control a deep water port where the Armada could anchor safely and wait for Parma's troops. This meant that the Armada was vulnerable to attack.

• The Spanish tactics were less effective. Their tactics relied on boarding, but the Spanish were unable to get close enough to the English vessels, because their ships were slower.

c) • Spain's leading admiral, Santa Cruz, died in February 1588. This meant the inexperienced Duke of Medina Sidonia led the Armada.

• The weather made it impossible for the Armada to return to the Channel after the battle at Gravelines. This meant that it had to flee to dangerous waters off Scotland and Ireland, where many ships sank or were wrecked.

2 • The threat from Spain was significantly reduced. Two more Armadas were sent in the 1590s, but they were unsuccessful.

• Victory over the Armada was an important step in England's development as a strong naval power to rival Spain. Improving its naval power helped England become richer by establishing more trade routes to India and the Far East, and contributed to England attempting to set up a colony in North America.

• Elizabeth became more popular due to the victory. It proved she was a capable monarch who was able to defend England from foreign invasion.

• The victory was seen as a sign that God was on the side of Protestantism, which strengthened the Protestant cause in England.

Pages 38-39 — Exam-Style Questions

1 Each aspect is marked separately and you can have a maximum of two marks per aspect. How to grade your answer:

• 1 mark for describing one credible aspect of the Ridolfi Plot in 1571.

• 2 marks for describing one credible aspect of the Ridolfi Plot in 1571 and using your own knowledge to support it.

Here are some points your answer may include:

• The plot was developed by an Italian banker called Roberto di Ridolfi. Ridolfi had played a part in the Revolt of the Northern Earls and used his Catholic contacts in England and the rest of Europe to organise the plot.

• The aim of the plot was to assassinate Elizabeth then arrange a marriage between Mary, Queen of Scots and the Duke of Norfolk. Mary would be made Queen of England. The plot was supported by the Pope, as well as King Philip II of Spain, who promised to provide men for a Spanish invasion of England.

• The plot was unsuccessful because the names of the conspirators were given to Elizabeth by her allies. Mary and the Duke of Norfolk were both implicated in the plot through letters that had been sent by Mary.

• Mary was not punished for her involvement in the plot, but her supervision in prison was made tighter. The Duke of Norfolk was arrested and executed.

2 This question is level marked. You should look at the level descriptions on page 58 to help you mark your answer. Here are some points your answer may include:

• Mary, Queen of Scots was executed because of her involvement in the Babington Plot. In this plot, Catholic conspirators planned to assassinate Elizabeth and make Mary queen instead. Mary was heavily involved in the plot — she sent a letter that directly approved plans to assassinate Elizabeth. This was enough to convince Elizabeth that she had no choice but to execute Mary.

Answers

- Mary had been involved in several plots to overthrow Elizabeth prior to the Babington Plot, including the Ridolfi Plot in 1571 and the Throckmorton Plot in 1583. This shows how determined Mary was to escape prison and make herself queen. The repeated nature of Mary's opposition to Elizabeth proved that Mary couldn't be trusted, so Elizabeth had her executed to avoid the possibility of another plot.
- Elizabeth had Mary, Queen of Scots executed because she posed a real threat to Elizabeth's rule. Mary was related to Margaret Tudor, and so had a legitimate claim to the English throne. This made her dangerous, because many people questioned Elizabeth's legitimacy, so Elizabeth was worried that people might overthrow her in favour of Mary.
- As a Catholic, Mary had the backing of the Pope and the Catholic Church. Once Elizabeth was excommunicated in 1570, many Catholics had to choose between following the orders of the Pope or obeying their queen. This meant there was potential for a Catholic uprising while Mary was still alive. After Mary was executed, the Catholic conspirators had no one to rally around, so their chances of overthrowing Elizabeth were weakened.
- Elizabeth drafted the Bond of Association in 1583, which required the execution of anyone who tried to overthrow Elizabeth. Once there was clear evidence that Mary was involved in the Babington Plot in 1587, Elizabeth had to execute her because she couldn't make an exception for her.

3 This question is level marked. You should look at the level descriptions on page 58 to help you mark your answer. Here are some points your answer may include:
- Bad weather throughout the Armada's invasion caused problems for the Spanish. The Armada was initially delayed by bad weather in the Bay of Biscay, then bad weather prevented it from returning to a strong defensive position at Calais after the English sent fireships to break up the Spanish ships. Finally, Atlantic storms around Scotland and Ireland caused many of the Spanish ships to be destroyed. These were all major setbacks for the Spanish and were down to luck because the Armada had no control over the weather.
- The English were lucky that Spain's leading admiral, Santa Cruz, died a few months before the invasion. This meant that the inexperienced Duke of Medina Sidonia had to lead the Armada, which meant that the Spanish leadership was weaker than it might have been.
- Francis Drake's raid on Cadiz in 1587 contributed significantly towards the defeat of the Armada. The attack damaged the Armada and delayed it by over a year, which gave England more time and money to prepare. This raid was successful because it was well planned and executed, not because of luck.
- Drake's raid weakened the Armada that eventually set sail in 1588. The capture of planks of seasoned wood during the raid forced the Spanish to use inferior, unseasoned wood to build their supply barrels. As a result, the Armada suffered from shortages of food and fresh water, which weakened Spanish morale. This was due to Drake's actions, rather than luck.

- The English used more effective tactics than the Spanish, allowing them to defeat the Armada in battle. The tactic of sending fireships to attack the Armada at Calais played a key role in the defeat of the Armada, as it forced the Spanish to flee their defensive position at Calais. The English also managed to stay out of range of the Spanish ships so that the Spanish couldn't board the English vessels and defeat them in hand-to-hand combat. This suggests that England's victory was due to their tactical strengths rather than luck.
- The Armada was seriously weakened by the actions of Dutch ships, which blockaded the Duke of Parma and prevented him from meeting up with the Armada at Dunkirk. This suggests that England managed to defeat the Spanish Armada because they were supported by the Dutch and because the Spanish plan to meet the Duke of Parma at Dunkirk was flawed from the beginning. Neither of these factors were due to luck.

4 Each aspect is marked separately and you can have a maximum of two marks per aspect. How to grade your answer:
- 1 mark for describing one credible aspect of the commercial rivalry between England and Spain.
- 2 marks for describing one credible aspect of the commercial rivalry between England and Spain and using your own knowledge to support it.

Here are some points your answer may include:
- The English economy relied on exports to Europe. Many of these went through the Dutch port of Antwerp. Spain ruled the Netherlands, so King Philip II could limit English access to Dutch ports like Antwerp.
- In 1568, Elizabeth took gold bullion from Spanish ships that had taken refuge in English ports to escape bad weather. Philip seized English ships in Antwerp and banned English trade with the Netherlands in response, damaging the English economy.
- Trade with Spain's colonies was potentially very profitable for England, but few Englishmen were granted a licence to trade with them. Instead, Elizabeth encouraged privateers to trade illegally with the Spanish colonies. These men also raided Spanish ships, stealing treasure that had been collected in the Americas.
- Elizabeth relied on the treasure stolen from Spanish ships by privateers for financial support. The privateers were supposed to be independent, so Elizabeth could claim that she wasn't responsible for their activities.
- England went to war with Spain in 1585 due to tension over the Spanish Netherlands. One of the main reasons why Elizabeth wanted to support Protestant rebels in the Netherlands was because of the importance of the Netherlands' ports for English trade.

5 This question is level marked. You should look at the level descriptions on page 58 to help you mark your answer. Here are some points your answer may include:
- A large number of northern nobles were Catholics. This meant that they wanted to restore Catholicism in England by placing a Catholic monarch on the throne. This encouraged them to support a revolt.
- Mary, Queen of Scots arrived in England in 1568. She had a legitimate claim to the throne because she was the granddaughter of Margaret Tudor and she was a Catholic, so many of the Catholic nobles in the north saw her arrival as an opportunity to have her recognised as Elizabeth's heir and so ensure that Elizabeth would be succeeded by a Catholic queen.

Answers

- The Earl of Northumberland was angry with Elizabeth because she had taken large areas of his land and shared them between his main rival in the north and a Protestant from the south. He was also angry that Elizabeth had claimed the profits from copper mines discovered on his estates. This made him more willing to support a revolt.
- The northern nobles resented the fact that their powers had been reduced by Elizabeth's use of the Council of the North to govern the region. To make matters worse, the Council of the North was dominated by southern Protestants.
- The northern nobles were worried that some of Elizabeth's advisors in the Privy Council, such as William Cecil, had become too powerful. They wanted to revolt in order to remove these advisors and replace them with men who would support their interests.

6   This question is level marked. You should look at the level descriptions on page 58 to help you mark your answer. Here are some points your answer may include:
- When the northern nobles revolted in 1569-1570, they had little support from the rest of the Catholic nobility and from ordinary people. Most Catholics chose to support Elizabeth over their religion, suggesting that Elizabeth's popularity as a ruler was enough to prevent the revolt from succeeding.
- One of the main reasons for the failure of the Revolt of the Northern Earls was that news of the Pope's decision to excommunicate Elizabeth arrived in England too late. If other Catholics had known of the Pope's support earlier, they might have supported the revolt. This suggests that poor timing and the actions of the Pope explain why the Revolt of the Northern Earls failed, rather than Elizabeth's popularity as a ruler.
- The Catholic plots to overthrow Elizabeth failed mainly because of Francis Walsingham's spy network, which proved effective in uncovering the plots against Elizabeth, such as the Throckmorton Plot and the Babington Plot, and gathering evidence against the main conspirators. This suggests that the plots failed because Walsingham made sure that Elizabeth was protected, not because she was a popular ruler.
- The failure of the Catholic plots was partly due to Philip II's reluctance to destroy his alliance with Elizabeth. He only supported the plots half-heartedly and rarely followed through on his promises because he didn't want to risk open conflict with England. Philip promised to send Spanish troops to help overthrow Elizabeth as part of the Ridolfi Plot and the Babington Plot, but never followed through on his promises. This suggests that Philip II's reluctance to fully support the plots played an important role in their eventual failure, regardless of whether or not Elizabeth was a popular ruler.

Elizabethan Society in the Age of Exploration, 1558-1588

Page 41 — Education

Knowledge and Understanding

1   a) Children were taught to behave correctly and given a basic religious education. Boys were taught work skills and girls helped their mothers with housework.
b) Pupils learned the Lord's Prayer, the 10 Commandments and the Creed.
c) Pupils learned basic reading and writing, and sometimes maths. They also learned about religion.
d) Pupils learned Latin and classical literature. Some of them also learned Greek.
e) Students studied advanced written and spoken Latin, Greek, arithmetic, music, astronomy, geometry and philosophy. After their undergraduate degree, they could specialise in law, theology or medicine.

2   Private tutors taught noble pupils how to behave in high society. They gave them the skills they would need to be successful at court.

3   Grammar schools were funded by wealthy individuals because there was no state education system.

4   Some boys from poorer backgrounds turned down places at grammar schools because their parents needed them to work at home.

Thinking Historically

1   a) The number of children who went to school increased.
b) The number of university students increased.
c) Books became cheaper and more widely available, which caused literacy levels to increase.

2   You can choose any option, as long as you explain your answer. For example:
The introduction of the printing press had the most significant effect on education in early Elizabethan England because it made education more accessible by making books much cheaper and more widely available. Changes such as the growing prosperity of the upper and middle classes and the need for a good education in certain careers only had an impact on a small section of society, whereas the printing press allowed more people to have access to education and increased literacy rates across the country.

3   a) • For — Religion was an important part of a pupil's learning from a very young age. Children were given a religious education at home and had to go to Sunday school, where they learned about Christianity. The lessons in petty schools also had a strong religious focus.
• Against — Young people learned about many things that weren't related to religion, especially as they grew older. For example, petty schools taught basic reading and writing, while grammar schools focused on Latin and classical literature. At university, students studied a wide range of subjects, from music to geometry.
b) • For — Girls were trained from a young age to help their mothers with household activities rather than learning literacy and numeracy. There were fewer girls than boys in petty schools and hardly any girls in grammar schools at all. Only boys were able to study at university.

Answers

- Against — Some girls did study at petty schools and grammar schools, where they might have received a good education by learning reading, writing, maths, Latin and classical literature. Some girls may also have been educated by private tutors.
  c) • For — Only a small proportion of Elizabethan children went to school — most poorer children learned work skills or household activities at home instead. Even when poorer boys were offered places at grammar schools, they were often unable to take them because they needed to help their parents at home. University was only accessible to richer families from the upper and middle classes.
  - Against — The number of children attending school in Elizabethan England was growing. Sunday schools and petty schools were open to children from both rich and poor families. Some grammar schools also offered free places to bright boys from poorer backgrounds, so it was possible for poor people to have access to some level of education.

Page 43 — Sports, Pastimes and the Theatre
Knowledge and Understanding
1 The royal court was a large group of people who travelled around with the Queen. Many of them took part in leisure activities with her. It was made up of over 1000 people, including servants, members of the Privy Council, nobles, ambassadors and foreign visitors.
2 Sports enjoyed by the rich:
   - hunting
   - hawking
   - fencing
   - tennis
   - bowls
   Sports enjoyed by the poor:
   - football
   - cockfighting
   - bull-baiting
   - bear-baiting
3 Poorer people had little time for leisure activities because they worked six days a week and then went to church on Sundays.
4 a) Before the 1570s, actors would travel around, performing in village squares or the courtyards of inns.
   b) The first theatres were built in London.
   c) Elizabethan theatres were usually round, open-air buildings. They had a raised stage that stretched out into the audience.
   d) Rich audience members sat under cover around the theatre's walls, whereas the poor audience members stood around the stage.
   e) The Queen's Men, The Admiral's Men and The Lord Chamberlain's Men.
5 Many theatres were built just outside the City of London in Southwark because the London authorities and many Puritans opposed the theatre. This is because they saw it as a source of crime and immorality.
6 • Acting companies needed the elite to pay for and promote their performances.
   • Acting companies needed the elite to protect them from opponents of the theatre.

Page 45 — Poverty
Knowledge and Understanding
1 • Food production couldn't keep pace with population growth, so there wasn't enough food to feed everyone.
   • In the 1550s and 1560s there were several poor harvests, which meant that less food was grown so there were food shortages.
   • Many landowners stopped growing grain and began sheep farming because it was more profitable for them. This meant that less food was grown so there were food shortages.
2 The Statute of Artificers set a maximum daily wage for skilled workers. This contributed to a rise in poverty because it prevented wages from rising when inflation caused the cost of living to increase.
3 a) Debasing the coinage means issuing coins that are made of cheaper metals instead of pure gold and silver. This made people believe that the coinage was worth less than before.
   b) Subsistence-level farming was a traditional farming method. Farmers rented strips of land in large open fields from landowners, and each farmer only grew enough crops to feed himself and his family. This method of farming was very inefficient.
   c) Enclosed farms were larger farms that were created when a landowner decided to stop sharing open fields between many farmers and enclose the land to create one large farm instead. They required fewer labourers than subsistence-level farms and were more efficient.
4 A vagabond was a migrant worker who left their village to look for work in towns and cities. The government was worried about the vagabondage because they thought it would encourage riots and rebellions.
Thinking Historically
1 a) • Food production couldn't keep up with population growth, so there were food shortages. This made the effect of the poor harvests in the 1550s and 1560s worse.
   • Population growth caused food prices to rise more quickly than wages because there wasn't enough food to feed everyone. This meant that many people could no longer afford to buy food.
   • There was growing competition for land as a result of population growth, so rents increased and fewer people could afford to rent land.
   b) • The development of enclosed farms meant that landowners needed fewer labourers to farm their land. This resulted in many farmers being evicted, leaving them unemployed and homeless.
   • Many farmers began sheep farming instead of growing grain, because exporting wool to Europe was very profitable. This meant that food prices rose because farmers weren't growing as much food.
   c) • Henry VIII's decision to debase the coinage meant that businessmen put their prices up. Rising prices were still a problem when Elizabeth became queen — it meant that many people couldn't afford to buy food.
   • Henry VIII closed down England's monasteries, which had been an important source of support for the poor, ill and disabled. These people were more likely to suffer from poverty after this support was taken away.

2   You can choose any option, as long as you explain your answer. For example:
Changes to agriculture had the most significant effect on poverty levels in early Elizabethan England because they made the food shortages and rising food prices caused by population growth and bad harvests worse. The development of enclosed farms meant that fewer labourers were needed on farms, so many people became homeless and unemployed. In addition to this, many landowners began farming sheep for wool rather than growing grain, so there was less food available when there was a bad harvest. This caused poverty levels to rise further because it meant that food prices increased so fewer people could afford to buy food.

3   • Population growth had a less significant effect on poverty levels because population growth might not have caused rising poverty levels if not for changes to agriculture and the limits to workers' wages caused by the Statute of Artificers. The growing population might have been able to continue feeding themselves through subsistence-level farming and buying other necessities if it weren't for these other changes.
    • The actions of Henry VIII had a less significant effect on poverty levels because the debasement of the coinage was already being tackled by 1560 and was only one of a number of reasons for rising prices. His decision to close down the monasteries meant that there was less support for poor people, but this didn't contribute to a rise in poverty levels.

Page 47 — Poverty
Knowledge and Understanding
1   Before the Elizabethan period, support for poor people came from organisations such as hospitals and monasteries. These were funded by rich people who made charitable donations.

2 a) People who were unable to support themselves, such as young orphans, the elderly, the sick and the disabled.
   b) People who wanted to work, but couldn't find a job in their home town or village.
   c) People who refused to work, such as beggars and criminals, as well as migrant workers who left their homes to travel around and find work.

3 a) • Magistrates were given the power to raise funds for poor relief. People who didn't pay were fined, but they could choose how much they contributed.
      • The undeserving poor could be publicly whipped.
   b) • Local officials were given the power to decide how much people should pay for poor relief.
      • The undeserving poor could be whipped or have a hole bored through their right ear, and repeat offenders could be imprisoned or even executed.

4   The money raised by the Poor Laws of 1563 and 1572 provided hospitals and housing for elderly, sick and disabled poor people. The money was used to make sure that poor children could be given apprenticeships of at least seven years, and the deserving poor benefited from work that local authorities were expected to provide under the laws.

Thinking Historically
1   Agree — The Poor Laws improved life for poor people in early Elizabethan England because they raised money which improved support for poor people. Elderly, sick and disabled people were able to go to hospital or were given housing that was paid for by taxes, poor children were given 7-year apprenticeships and local governments provided work for the deserving poor.
    Disagree — However, the poor laws only benefited the helpless and deserving poor. People who were believed to be 'undeserving' faced harsher punishments following the introduction of the Poor Laws, such as being whipped or sent to prison. The 'undeserving poor' included 'vagabonds', many of whom were just poor people trying to find work.

2   For:
    • An increase in poverty and crime rates led the government to believe that the poor might rise up in rebellion if poverty wasn't addressed. Maintaining law and order was the government's main concern, not poverty itself.
    • Many people believed that criminals and vagabonds had encouraged the Revolt of the Northern Earls in 1569. The government used the Poor Laws to discourage people from being involved in any future rebellions by introducing harsh punishments.
    Against:
    • The government genuinely wanted to help poor people who they thought were 'deserving' — naming them the deserving poor showed that the government felt that these people were entitled to help.
    • Taxes raised from Poor Laws provided hospitals and housing for the helpless poor, such as the elderly and the disabled. The helpless poor weren't likely to rebel, but the government tried to help them anyway.

Page 49 — Exploration and Discovery
Knowledge and Understanding
1   By 1558, Spain and Portugal had explored Africa, Asia and the Americas, as well as establishing many colonies in the Americas.

2   Before 1561, English sailors used coastal features to navigate. This made it impossible for them to cross oceans because they couldn't sail into open water.

3 a) In 1561, 'The Art of Navigation' by Martin Cortés was translated from Spanish into English. This gave English sailors information on how to use a sea astrolabe to navigate.
   b) From the 1570s, English sailors began using the log and line, which helped them estimate their speed more accurately.

4   • Ships were faster.
    • Ships were more stable.
    • Ships were easier to navigate.
    • Ships were better-suited to ocean voyages.
    • Ships could carry larger cargoes, making them more profitable.

Answers

5   A monopoly is when a group of merchants is given exclusive rights to trade in a particular part of the world. The Spanish Company had a monopoly on English trade with Spain's colonies.

Thinking Historically

1
- Spain controlled Antwerp and made it difficult for English merchants to export goods like woollen cloth through the port and into Europe. This encouraged English merchants to find other international trade routes.
- The commercial and political rivalry between the two countries encouraged Elizabeth to compete with Spain globally, as well as in Europe. She sanctioned long-distance trade and privateering.
- The rivalry with Spain also led Elizabeth to encourage explorers to seek opportunities to establish a colony in the Americas.

2   You can choose either option as long as you explain your answer. For example:

Agree — The rivalry with Spain was the most significant reason why there was an increase in exploration. Spain's control of Antwerp meant that English sailors needed to find alternative overseas trading posts in order to keep exporting woollen cloth. In addition, Elizabeth wanted to rival Spain's overseas empire, so she sanctioned voyages to America to explore opportunities to set up English colonies.

Disagree — The development of new technology was the most significant reason why there was an increase in English exploration. England wanted to rival Spain globally, but this wouldn't have been possible unless English sailors had access to technology that allowed them to make long journeys across oceans. Developments like the sea astrolabe and the log and line were essential for allowing English sailors to successfully navigate across oceans like the Spanish and Portuguese had been doing since the 1400s.

Page 51 — Exploration and Discovery

Knowledge and Understanding

1
- They were attracted to illegal trade with Spanish colonies, which could be very profitable.
- They hoped to profit from establishing English colonies in the region.

2   Sailors hoped to trade in silk and spices directly with Asia. They wanted to cut out merchants in Venice, who acted as middlemen, dominating trade with Asia and keeping prices high.

3
- They tried to find the North West Passage around the top of North America.
- Some sailed through the Mediterranean and went overland to India.

4 a) Drake successfully explores the South American coast, raiding many Spanish settlements.

   b) He sails around the southern tip of South America before capturing two extremely valuable Spanish treasure ships near Lima. This means he has to return home by a different route — Spain had sent ships to intercept him and recover the treasure.

   c) Drake sails north along the North American coast, possibly looking for the North West Passage so he can sail around the top of North America and back across the Atlantic.

   d) After failing to find the passage, Drake sails west across the Pacific to Indonesia. One of the captured ships has people with experience of crossing the Pacific, as well as charts for the journey. This makes the journey a lot safer.

5   Elizabeth recognises Drake's achievements by knighting him. This encourages other sailors to go on more long-distance journeys in the hope of gaining similar royal recognition.

Thinking Historically

1   For:
- Many sailors explored the Americas in order to find economic opportunities. They wanted to trade illegally with Spanish settlements and raid Spanish treasure ships. Some hoped to get rich by establishing colonies.
- In the 1570s, English sailors explored different routes to Asia because of the economic opportunity to trade in silk and spices. Some sailors tried to find the North West Passage, while others travelled to the Mediterranean and then overland to India.
- As the Spanish made it increasingly difficult to export goods through Antwerp, English merchants explored new routes in search of new trading opportunities.

Against:
- People also sailed long distances in search of fame and glory. Francis Drake's knighthood after his voyage around the world encouraged some people to explore not just for wealth, but for royal recognition.
- England's rivalry with Spain also contributed to exploration. Elizabeth encouraged English sailors to establish colonies overseas in order to rival Spain's global expansion.

2   You can choose either option as long as you explain your answer. For example:

Expedition to the Spanish and Portuguese coast:
- This expedition was more important to Elizabeth's reign because it actively contributed to securing her position as Queen. If Drake hadn't attacked Cadiz, the Armada would have been able to set off over a year earlier and Spanish morale would have been much higher. This would have made the Armada more dangerous and given England less time to prepare its defences.
- The expedition also led to the capture of the *San Filipe*, a Spanish treasure ship. This paid for Drake's raid and helped pay for England's defences against the Armada.

Circumnavigation of the world:
- Circumnavigating the world was far more remarkable than the raid on Cadiz. Drake was only the second man in the world to manage it, and the first Englishman.
- Drake's circumnavigation earned him a knighthood. This encouraged further exploration from sailors looking for similar fame and recognition.

Page 53 — Raleigh and Virginia

Knowledge and Understanding

1   New Albion, in California, and Newfoundland, in eastern Canada.

2
- An English colony could act as a base for attacking Spanish treasure ships.
- Establishing an English colony would allow England to challenge Spanish dominance in the Americas.
- It was hoped that a colony would provide raw materials and be useful in future wars with Spain.

Answers

3 Raleigh named Virginia after Elizabeth, who was known as the 'Virgin Queen'.

4 1584 — Raleigh sends a fact-finding mission to North America. The mission explores Roanoke Island, returning to England with two Native Americans who give a glowing report of the region. This encourages Raleigh to organise a second expedition.

1585 — Raleigh sends five ships to Virginia under the command of Sir Richard Grenville. 108 settlers ('planters') establish a colony on Roanoke, and Grenville goes back to England for more supplies.

1586 — Francis Drake visits Roanoke. Grenville is yet to return with supplies, so most of the planters return to England with Drake, leaving only a few behind to maintain the colony.

1587 — A third expedition goes to Roanoke, but finds it deserted. The men left behind in 1586 may have been killed by local people. Around 100 planters settle on Roanoke to rebuild the colony.

1588 — The planters are expecting further supplies, but the supply ships are delayed because of the Spanish Armada.

1590 — The supply ships eventually make it to Roanoke, but all of the planters are gone.

Thinking Historically

1 Your table could include the following points:
- Point — The Roanoke colony failed because poor planning meant there was a lack of supplies.
  Evidence — Successive expeditions to Roanoke Island failed to take enough supplies with them, so the organisers of the expeditions clearly didn't learn their lesson.
  Why evidence supports point — This contributed to the failure of the Roanoke colony because it meant that on both occasions when the planters tried to build a colony, they didn't have enough supplies to survive until ships returned came from England. This was due to poor planning because the same mistakes were made on multiple occasions.
- Point — The planters were unlucky. It was bad luck that the 1587/1588 expedition coincided with the attack of the Spanish Armada.
  Evidence — In 1588, around 100 planters on the island were expecting supply ships, but the fleet was delayed by the Spanish Armada. When the fleet finally reached the colony, all of the planters had disappeared.
  Why evidence supports point — Roanoke was difficult to colonise, and the planters needed supplies to reach them quickly to have a chance of succeeding. However, the supply ships were delayed because of the attack of the Spanish Armada, which came at an unlucky time for the organisers of the expedition.
- Point — The failure of the colony was partly down to attacks from the local population.
  Evidence — When a third expedition reached Roanoke in 1587, all of the planters who had stayed behind in 1586 had gone missing. It is assumed that they were attacked and killed by local people. The same thing happened to around 100 planters who tried to rebuild the colony.
  Why evidence supports point — If the native population of Roanoke had not attacked the planters, it is possible that the colony would have survived until supplies arrived.

Pages 56-57 — Exam-Style Questions

1 Each aspect is marked separately and you can have a maximum of two marks per aspect. How to grade your answer:
- 1 mark for describing one credible aspect of university education in early Elizabethan England.
- 2 marks for describing one aspect and using your own knowledge to support it.
Here are some points your answer may include:
- There were two English universities, Oxford and Cambridge. Some boys went to study at these universities after leaving grammar school.
- The number of university students increased during Elizabeth's reign. This was due to the growing prosperity of the upper and middle classes.
- University courses were mostly conducted in Latin. Students would study advanced written and spoken Latin.
- In later years of university, students would study arithmetic, music, Greek, astronomy, geometry and philosophy. They could specialise in law, theology or medicine after completing an undergraduate degree.

2 This question is level marked. You should look at the level descriptions on page 58 to help you mark your answer. Here are some points your answer may include:
- Noblemen and courtiers were expected to be skilled at certain sports, such as fencing, in order to succeed at court. As a result, many rich people practised these sports from a young age because this helped them to succeed in society.
- Some sports, such as hawking, tennis and bowls, were only available to rich people because they required expensive equipment. Elizabeth was particularly fond of hawking, but keeping and training falcons was an expensive hobby.
- Most ordinary people worked six days a week and spent Sunday in church, so they didn't have as much time for leisure activities as the social elite. However, they often enjoyed sports and pastimes on festival days.
- Rich and poor people had a different experience of the theatre, because rich people could afford better seats. Rich people sat under cover around the theatre's walls, whereas poorer people couldn't afford covered seating so they had to stand throughout the performance.

3 This question is level marked. You should look at the level descriptions on page 58 to help you mark your answer. Here are some points your answer may include:
- Drake was only the second man to ever successfully sail around the world, and the first Englishman to do so. His circumnavigation of 1577-80 was an important contribution to English exploration as it paved the way for other English sailors as it showed that global exploration was possible.
- Drake returned from his circumnavigation with lots of Spanish treasure that he'd captured from two valuable treasure ships near Lima. The wealth he brought back from the journey encouraged other sailors to go on similar voyages of discovery, so he contributed to global exploration by showing how profitable exploration could be.
- Queen Elizabeth contributed to exploration by encouraging English sailors to trade overseas. For example, in 1577 she gave a group of merchants called the Spanish Company a monopoly on English trade with Spain's colonies. This may have inspired other explorers to profit from overseas trade.

Answers

- Elizabeth also encouraged exploration by recognising the achievements of English sailors publicly — she knighted Francis Drake after his circumnavigation of the world. Therefore, Elizabeth contributed to English exploration by making it seem prestigious.
- Elizabeth also contributed to global exploration by giving Walter Raleigh permission to explore and colonise unclaimed territories in North America. This led to the establishment of the Roanoke colony in Virginia. This shows that Elizabeth encouraged sailors to visit new lands.
- Walter Raleigh and Richard Grenville contributed to the global exploration, even though their attempts to colonise Virginia failed. They had some success in establishing the Roanoke colony, but were unlucky that the colony failed to survive. Their work may still have been useful to other explorers who planned to establish colonies.

4 Each aspect is marked separately and you can have a maximum of two marks per aspect. How to grade your answer:
- 1 mark for describing one credible aspect of government policies in early Elizabethan England.
- 2 marks for describing one aspect and using your own knowledge to support it.

Here are some points your answer may include:
- Government policies towards the poor were based on splitting poor people into three groups: the helpless poor, the deserving poor and the undeserving poor. Most policies were designed to aid the helpless poor and the deserving poor, but they punished the undeserving poor, who were seen as a threat to society.
- The government started to introduce taxes to raise money for the poor. Previously, support from the poor had come from charitable donations made by rich people.
- The 1563 Poor Law allowed local magistrates to raise funds for poor relief and to fine people who refused to pay. However, the law didn't state how much each person was supposed to contribute.
- The 1572 Poor Law allowed local officials to decide how much people should pay. There was a national system of taxation to pay for poor relief by the end of the century.
- The taxes raised by the government's Poor Laws were spent on hospitals and housing for the elderly, sick and disabled. The local authorities were supposed to find work for the deserving poor, while poor children were given apprenticeships.

5 This question is level marked. You should look at the level descriptions on page 58 to help you mark your answer. Here are some points your answer may include:
- Sir Richard Grenville left 108 planters on Roanoke Island in 1585 and promised to return with supplies. However, when Drake landed on the island in 1586, Grenville still hadn't returned and the planters were almost out of supplies. Drake took most of the men back to England with him. The lack of proper supplies was an important reason why the first attempt to establish a colony failed.
- It is believed that many of the settlers who attempted to establish a colony in Virginia were killed by local people. When the third expedition arrived on Roanoke Island in 1587, the men who had been left behind by Drake had disappeared. This meant that the attempts to form a colony had to be started again. The planters who were left on Roanoke Island in 1587 also disappeared by the time supply ships reached them in 1590. The threat posed by native people was therefore an important reason why Raleigh's attempts to colonise Virginia failed.
- The planters who attempted to settle on Roanoke Island in 1585 and 1587 found it difficult to grow food on Roanoke. This meant that they were heavily dependent on receiving supplies from England. The difficulty of growing food on Roanoke Island was a major reason why the attempts to colonise Virginia failed, since the colony could not support itself.
- The attack of the Spanish Armada in 1588 delayed the delivery of supplies, which the planters were dependent on. This meant that all of the planters who came to Roanoke Island in 1587 died because supplies didn't reach them until 1590.
- Raleigh's attempts to colonise Virginia were poorly planned. Initial exploration of Roanoke was inadequate because the planters were unaware of many of the problems of settling on Roanoke Island, such as the difficulty of growing crops. The project was badly organised from the beginning. A major reason for this was that Raleigh's funding was limited. As a result, poor planning and organisation was an important reason for the failure to establish a colony.

Answers

6   This question is level marked. You should look at the level
     descriptions on page 58 to help you mark your answer. Here
     are some points your answer may include:
     • The population increased rapidly during Elizabeth's reign
        from around 3 million people to over 4 million. This
        led to food shortages, because food production didn't
        keep up with the demands of the growing population.
        This caused food prices to rise and resulted in poverty
        because people couldn't afford to eat.
     • Population growth caused the standard of living to fall,
        because prices for food and other goods rose faster than
        wages. This was made worse by the Statute of Artificers,
        which set a maximum daily wage for some workers.
        As a result, many workers could no longer afford basic
        necessities and were pushed into poverty.
     • Population growth meant that more people had to
        compete for land. This caused rents to rise, making land
        less affordable and putting more financial pressure on
        those who were already struggling.
     • New farming techniques like enclosure reduced the
        number of farmers who were needed to farm the land,
        as farmers combined small strips of land into larger
        farms that were more efficient. This resulted in many
        farmers being evicted, leading to unemployment and
        homelessness among the poorer members of society.
     • Many landowners stopped growing grain and started to
        farm sheep instead, since exporting wool to Europe was
        more profitable than selling grain. This added to the
        problem of poverty, as it made food shortages worse by
        reducing the amount of grain available to buy in England,
        meaning that the grain that was available cost more to
        buy.
     • Poor harvests in the 1550s and 1560s made poverty even
        more extreme, because it meant that there was less food
        available to feed England's growing population. Food
        prices rose as a result of these shortages.
     • Traditionally, monasteries had provided support for poor,
        ill and disabled people. However, Henry VIII had closed
        down England's monasteries, so there was little support
        for the increasing number of people who needed it.
     • Henry VIII had debased the coinage by putting cheaper
        metals into coins that had been pure gold or silver. This
        made the coins less valuable, causing inflation because
        businessmen increased their prices. As a result, when
        Elizabeth came to power, prices were still too high for
        poor people to afford, so poverty levels rose.

Index

HFFAO41